Ms. Cheevious
IN
HOLLYWOOD

My zany years spent working in Tinsel Town.

LISA JEY DAVIS

Knowledge Is Power Publishing
Santa Monica

Copyright © 2014 by Lisa Jey Davis
Cover, Title Page and other professional photos courtesy of Lindsay Rosenberg Photography

All rights reserved under International and Pan-American Copyright Conventions.
Published by Knowledge is Power Publishing, Santa Monica, California.

Drift Away
Words and Music by Mentor Williams
Copyright © 1972 ALMO MUSIC CORP.
Copyright Renewed
All Rights Reserved Used by Permission
Reprinted by Permission of Hal Leonard Corporation

Knowledge Is Power Publishing, website address:
www.knowledgeispowerpublishing.com
First Edition

This book (and my life) is dedicated to my two boys Graden and Joel. Through all the storms we faced, you unwittingly made every decision extremely important, gave me purpose and drive beyond my ability, and made any memory I now cherish eternal. Without knowing or trying, you were always able to bring me back to earth and reel me back in to the stuff that really matters. And despite any lemons we were served, I feel like together we made the BEST DAMN LEMONADE EVER! I love you both more than you'll ever be able to fathom.

I have far too many life quotes, because I'm just that kind of person. But hopefully this will sum up for you the wild ride you are about to read:

"I am not afraid of storms, for I am learning how to sail my ship."
Louisa May Alcott

Author's Note:

This book is a memoir, not an autobiography, covering a period of time when I was a newly divorced single mom trying to make it in Hollywood—or really, trying to find a way to live large and in charge despite the odds (and sowing some wild oats in the process). It is a depiction of *my* memories, which probably differ from other's recollections of the same events. All dialogue is approximate because my memory, while often compared to a steel trap, falls short more than I like to admit. Also, most of the names of the people I worked and played with while managing celebrities for various television shows and events have been changed, with the exception of the celebrities and a friend or two. All of this was done to protect the privacy of those I know and love. At times during my story, I step aside to offer some words of wisdom learned during my adventure, because dammit, who tells single moms these things? When I do so, that section will appear indented.

Acknowledgements

It would be wrong to start this book without thanking the key figures in my world who have made me who I am today: My two boys—For all you've put up with over the years. To Joel, who, although you weren't too keen on my decision to talk about your teen years as seen through my own lens, you're a truly beautiful person, and by allowing this to be a part of *my* journey have shown just how cool you are. And Graden, though you've lived with your dad for several years, you're still my baby, and I am so proud of you and how you are growing into adulthood. Despite my goofy missteps and glaring mistakes, you both will always be my little boys who make me so proud. You boys and me, baby! That's what really matters. I love you both more than life.

To my loving man and my domestic "pahhhdnuhhhh," Tom Schanley. (series!) I am so grateful to you my love, for the incredible amount of effort, time, heart, soul and wit you devoted to me and to this project. I thought you would puke if you had to read the same damn chapter one more time, and yet you always did, and you always came through big. When I asked you to read the entire *book* all over again after multiple edits, I cringed, but once again you were wonderful. You read it and still came back with more ideas. You helped me add razor-sharp wit and clarity to my story (I mean, '*black belt effort not to burst out laughing?*' Come on!), and… well, thank you. I couldn't have done it without your unending loving support, and your willingness to relinquish copious amounts of time with me to the Big Screen. And when that three picture deal and unrelenting work as an actor kicks into high gear, you know I'm your girl, and I will support you in everything you do. But thank you, thank you, thank you. I love you.

I'd like to thank my wonderful friends and family members, Britt (my cohort, colleague and more of a sister than a best friend), Bogey and Bacall, Lori Neal, Gina Sirico, my niece (and author) H. Raven Rose, my niece and surrogate daughter Risse Miller, the lovely Teri Smieja and members of my author's networking group on Facebook, Scott Bury (my final editor), Onisha Ellis and Anne Marie Klein for reading my book and giving me your invaluable impressions and insights. I appreciated (and took to heart) your ideas, many of which are represented in the finished product. Love you people!

To my lovely sisters:

Judy (Sherwood Narveson)—Your unending support in commenting on the blog, and in creating graphics for Ms. Cheevious, for my websites, my book proposals, products, every project I could ever concoct, has been a blessing I can never repay, though I hope to be able to one day. Thank you so very much. I'm so lucky you're in my life, and that you don't mind whipping out a quick graphic now and then!

Jackie (Sherwood Van Hauen)—Thank you so much for your unending support through the years, posting comments on the MsCheevious.com blog, "liking" posts on the Ms. Cheevious facebook page (and on my author page), and showing support in so many other ways.

Susan (Sherwood Parr)—You have been a moral support and encourager from day one. Your love and time involved supporting me is immeasurable. I am so lucky that all of you, my sisters who are still alive and kicking today, are in my life.

Mimi (Sherwood Larimore)— I miss you so deeply. You were going to get me into Oprah's Book Club, and you thought I rocked!! If it hadn't been for your encouragement about my writing, I never would have finished this book. I mean that sincerely. I will never forget the love, laughter and excitement you brought to my life.

And finally to my mom—You modeled the essential cool for me as a mother. You were the quintessential Ms. Cheevious. I love you, mom. See you again one day!

Contents

Introduction — Milf And Cookies 1
One — If I'd Attacked Him He'd Be Dead 7
Two — Mommy Needs A Makeover 24
Three — Bring Me A Mint Julep 39
Four — And They're Off! 50
Five — Fit To Be Tied…Up 58
Six — Project Runway Could Be My Bitch 65
Seven — The "M" In Milf Stands For "Mother" 71
Eight — The Great Waify Boob Conspiracy 80
Nine — Let's Get This Party Started 88
Ten — My Son The Homeless Guy 102
Eleven — It Was A Super Jambalaya 111
Twelve — And The Grammy Goes To … 129
Thirteen — It's Raining Men 143
Fourteen — How I Saved Aerosmith From
    Ms. Bitchy Bitch Bitch From Bitchville 153
Fifteen — Jack The Dripper 172
Sixteen — Mother Is Not A Four Letter Word 193
About The Author 205
Single Mom Resources 209

Milf And Cookies

"It's a whole thing! You know! You really didn't see American Pie?" —Married MILF-Chaser Guy

"Oh, you're definitely a MILF!" he said, as if to explain the little acronym he'd just laid on me. After a pause, he added glibly, "You know, Mother I'd Love to Fuck?" certain that I must have heard the phrase before.

Pause.

Pause.

"Didn't you see *American Pie*?"

No. Of course I hadn't. Why *would* I have? I wasn't sure whether to be insulted (a *definite* "lean toward") or flattered (a not-so-definite) by this.

"NO WAY! Nobody calls women that!" The name I'd just been given was still sinking in. "You're kidding me, aren't you?"

"No, I mean it!" he said with a proud-to-know-I've-taught-her-this grin. "It's a whole thing. You know! You really didn't see *American Pie*?"

"No, I really didn't," I said, laughing, enjoying the exchange but with a look of utter disgust on my face. "I *cannot* believe anyone is really looking for mothers to 'fuck,' let alone calling them that!" The more I thought about it, the more incensed I became.

I didn't realize it at the time, but I came away from that conversation a changed person. You just can't un-hear that shit. I had to consider the source, I suppose; a married man interested in MILFs. Of *course* he knew what they were. He skated along life's edge as part of his everyday routine. But, over the next few hours, days and weeks, the bulbs started lighting up all over my brain. Didn't it seem, since the divorce, that I was getting an awful lot of attention from some inordinately young guys? *Like that cute bellhop at the little hotel in Long Beach.* He couldn't have been more than twenty. He was overly helpful and obviously interested. *So that's why he stood there gaping, mouth open and salivating!*

Then there was the young, good-looking guy at the dry cleaners, the one whose dad owned the place, who seemed more into surfing than working. He always handed me my laundry, never charged me for my dress shirts, all with a wink and a smile, of course. *Did he really think he had a shot?* I don't know, but who was I to complain, if there was free dry cleaning involved?

Oh… and the energetic young lawyer who remembered meeting me at some party and had been interested in knowing me ever since. He saw me at my favorite coffee shop once and later confessed he made it his regular stop so he could meet me. I probably would've been flattered if it weren't for being creeped out by his stalking me. It was all coming back now.

I had certainly come a long way. I'd been married not too long before to a mentally and verbally abusive man who had no idea how to love or be intimate and who at the time, always had to feel as though he was as good as, better than or superior to me and others around him. He seemed to make it his mission to let me know how inadequate, unappealing, and unattractive I was, and how unhappy and dissatisfied he was.

I came away from that failed twelve-year marriage feeling fat, frumpy, ugly and in need of some serious change. Losing weight became a major goal in my life, because I knew all too well what it was like to be lean, trim and athletic, and I knew that I liked it. Sadly, I'd come to the place where I also knew what life was like to *not* be lean. I dealt with an inordinate amount of joint issues from athletic injuries and other freak goings-on with my body since gaining the extra weight during and after my last pregnancy. It was not a pleasant existence. I'd been fit before, and I determined to get there again. My determination became extreme, because that is how I get things done in my life.

But I was not ready for the onslaught of propositions that came once I decided to give myself some much-needed attention. *It's amazing what a strict diet, updated wardrobe, highlights and haircut can do for a gal! Divorce was good for me!*

Still, I was surprised at this whole MILF concept. I typed it into an Internet search box once and was immediately blasted with porn. As someone who'd learned how to navigate computers and learned everything in DOS (one of the first personal computer operating systems, before anyone ever knew what a computer mouse was) from the age of twelve, and had graduated along with everyone else to Windows, I knew all too well this meant I'd opened up my computer to dreaded Internet cookies (about *MILFS*, people)! Me—a single mom with school-age kids!

I quickly wiped my computer clean, eliminating all browser history. I did anything else I could think of, including erasing files and reinstalling my Internet browser software to remove all trace of my fleeting curiosity.

Once I knew that someone saw me as a single "hot" mom, it seemed that everyone knew, as if a beacon were fastened to my forehead or something. Potential suitors came out of the woodwork. People would find out that I had a child in his late teens and immediately start with the incessant questioning:

"Do your son's friends think you're hot? Do they call you a MILF?" *I'm sorry, what?!*

"Are all your other mom-friends hot, too?" *Oh, please!*

A bartender friend asked me if my son's friends tried to hit on me. *"Thanks for the milk & cookies, Mrs. D. Whatcha doin' Saturday?"* No, none of them ever said that, and oh.my.god! What a relief!

The truth is, young guys weren't dissuaded by the fact that I had a son close to their age. Nope. Instead, they would muster up their smoothest, "That's cool. You're a *total* MILF, dude! You're hot!" And yes, they'd actually say, "Dude."

Still, it was part of my nature to embark on a mission of discovery after the divorce drop-kicked me back into single motherhood. I remembered the sting I'd felt when I attended my first Mother's Day brunch with another single-mother girlfriend, only to be met with awkward stares and pitiful glances from happy families. I had to investigate this thing that screamed something other than the norm—something that seemed to shatter the stereotypes. For too many years I'd struggled with the choices offered by conventional American motherhood: one that embraced den and room mothers, soccer moms and PTA members (all great and enviable positions, don't get me wrong), but was hard-pressed to encourage a mother with intelligence or creativity to contribute other great things to society. Not that I believed myself to possess such traits at the time, no. I was simply looking for, but not finding alternatives to the traditional symbols of American motherhood.

Think about it. Even when mothers such as Michelle Obama, Gloria Estefan, Hillary Clinton or Jacqueline Kennedy Onassis are applauded or respected for their intelligence and societal contributions, it is always within a specific framework of feminine frailty, as *the wife* of someone, or *the mother* of someone else, or simply a *female* bringing the *womanly* perspective—though some women have worked to change or are changing this, such as Margaret Thatcher or even Angelina Jolie. There is no getting around those female body parts that give away our identity. Once that identity is revealed, well, we're destined to adjusted reactions to our contributions. And where *do* we *single* mothers fit into this picture of conventional motherhood? How are we supposed to be den mothers and soccer moms and still support our families?

These old-fashioned and outmoded ideas and social mores are fading slowly, but still the notion of a mother having more to offer society and the world outside the home, or in addition to what she does at home, somehow seems to threaten the mainline institution of American motherhood, not to mention the rest of society. They don't seem to know what to do with us.

I knew I was an excellent mother, as my therapists and many of my friends attested and still tell me today. I wasn't necessarily looking for a new identity for myself as a mother and certainly, if I were, it would not have been a MILF.

I wasn't too bothered by the notion that others thought I was "hot," but I was *more* interested in finding (or creating) a brand new look for myself than what conventional American motherhood offered.

While living and experiencing the single/dating life in Los Angeles, I had so many crazy, hilarious experiences and interactions. Yes, OK, sometimes with younger guys. I just knew these stories would not rest until I put them in writing.

My decision to write this book came in part because I had not only experienced some AWESOME and enviable moments, but I'd come through some extremely difficult situations—the kind that end up on the front page of the newspaper with headlines like, "Estranged husband returns to murder wife and children." I really did feel fortunate to get out alive and (somewhat) sane (or not). But I truthfully had no idea of the huge and wonderful world that waited for me as a healthy, happy woman.

When I started to write this book, I attended a writer's conference where the speakers prodded me to establish myself and develop a platform for my writing. The primary way they suggested to accomplish that was to write a blog. I took them up on it. I began a humorous blog, MsCheevious.com—named after the book, of course—sharing hints of my life following the events written here. The blog provided a way to bring my zany world to an audience in 2-D and strives to inspire other single moms to kick ass and take names—or at minimum, it distracts them from the impossible demands on their daily lives. It has grown and changed some over the years, but it is still ever so "Ms. Cheevious."

Between the covers here are some of the stories that make me who I am today. There are infuriating tests of my character and real-life examples of how I overcame them. There are funny tales that could have been taken directly from the *I Love Lucy* show. And there are stories of working, flouncing and cavorting about with friends, (celebrities, entertainment industry folks, and others) in Hollywood, many of which seem unbelievable and sometimes enviable. But before taking you there, I reach back in time and introduce you to a profoundly influential individual in my life. My ex-husband is the one human being who, unbeknownst to him, helped make my television, writing and public relations careers a reality. When we met and married we were very young. We were fun-loving and really enjoyed the good times we had with our friends and family. But the truth is we were never in love. I don't believe we really knew what it was to be in love. And when the drug relapses started and we both struggled to keep things together in our own way, things simply unraveled and crumbled to pieces. Were it not for his final drug relapse, the relapse that ended our marriage, I may not have pursued my dreams, much less seen them become reality.

I hope my story provides inspiration and encouragement for the hot mamas of the world (and we humans are *all* hot in our own way, mothers or not), trying to find their way in this big, bad, beautiful world. I truly hope you enjoy the reading as much as I enjoyed the writing.

If I'd Attacked Him He'd Be Dead

"I wonder if Scarlett Johansson can tell I escaped insanity to be here."

"Lisa Jey!" Aaron, my friend and boss called into the headset, "I need you to get Scarlett Johansson and take her to prompter! She's hung up at red carpet somewhere. Over!" *Kkkhhh.*

"I'm on it," I replied. *Hmm ... I saw Lost in Translation ... I'll recognize her,* I thought. But as I opened the sound stage door, I was met by a barrage of equipment and people: celebrities drinking and chatting, production crews maneuvering cameras and boom microphones and journalists, all crammed together outside the backstage door. I had to get through this cluster just to get to the red carpet and I had to move fast. *Okay, this may not be so easy.*

I pushed my way authoritatively through the crowd, without prejudice. "People! Hello! Can—you—please—MOVE? It's imperative I get through now! Snoop Dogg? Hi. I'm sorry! No time to talk here. I have! To get! To red! Carpet!"

I finally spilled out of the other side of the crowd near the opposite end of the red carpet nearly tripping over my own stilettos (I always dress up for show time). Behind me lay party mayhem. In front of me were scattered miscellaneous faces in utter silence. It was like night and day. Where was everyone? And where was Scarlett? I scanned the landscape frantically, looking for someone who might know my charge. A few guys wearing baggie jeans with boxers exposed, black shades, sports jerseys and tons of gold bling were talking on cell phones and slouching against the audience stands. *Rappers… Why do they all dress alike?* I walked up to one of them, who had his phone up to his ear and asked, "Have you seen Scarlett Johansson?" He said nothing, but pointed to his right and looked over toward a skinny little thing who was smiling and chatting away, seemingly amused by the mayhem behind me. She looked fabulous in a black little bustier dress and yellow mesh tank. Her hair looked like it was pulled up in these tiny sort-of chop-stick things.

I walked over to her, conjuring up my most cheerful voice and said, "Hey there! I need to get you to prompter pretty quickly. They're waiting for you."

"Okay," she answered with a smile and followed me. This time, the chaotic crowd seemed like no big deal. I knew it was for one reason only: I had Scarlett with me. The friggin' Red Sea parted because everyone wanted a piece of—I mean a glance at Scarlet Johansson.

As we worked our way through, Scarlet kept pausing to greet every single person along the way she seemed to know, and there were a ton. *This is not good.* Finally the stage door came into view, and just as I was starting to feel my breath recalibrate, Scarlett stopped dead in her tracks and began a full-on conversation with an unassuming guy who was standing there in a tan leather jacket and dark sunglasses. I had no idea how she knew him, or why anyone would assume it was okay to hold things up, but he was smiling a lot and looked pretty happy. I just didn't get it. I would have burst into flames, but my appreciation and enthusiasm for all things fun and social (not to mention the fact that I kept getting involved in Scarlett's little conversations, laughing and smiling right along with her and her "friends") kept me somewhat cool. I couldn't tell whether any of them saw through my clever producer disguise. I found I was pretty adept at waxing professional and not letting on about anything that had gone on in my life. But it was in those moments, attempting to relate to people who were on the red carpet, and who knew Scarlett for one reason or another, that I couldn't help but wonder if they saw "Damaged" or "Been through hell" written all over my face. Was there any chance Scarlett saw past the headset into the chaotic, heartbreaking world I'd come from? Could she possibly see that I'd been through the horrors of my husband's violent drug addiction, the threat of losing my kids and going to jail, and had suffered deeply seeing my older son under someone else's care? I hoped not, as I chuckled and smiled as knowingly as possible at their talk of designer gowns or shoes, or the party they'd been to in Cannes. I watched as she and this mystery guy laughed together for all on the sidelines to see.

After a few minutes, I was jolted back again. *Kkkhhh.* "Lisa Jey! Where's Scarlett?! Over!" *Kkkhhh.*

Trying to talk under my breath I mumbled into the headset "I've got her. We're at the stage door. But there's a hold-up."

"What?" Aaron commanded. In that second I noticed a boom mic hanging over my head and with a glance over my shoulder saw an entire MTV camera crew behind me, trying to capture all of this on film. Why is everyone making such a big deal about this?

Then, Mr. Unassuming reached out, shook my hand and said, "Hi. How're you doing?"

Oh. I get it now.

"I'm good, thanks!" I said cheerily. "So, *you* were the Tom they were looking for earlier?" I said, laughing to Mr. Unassuming *Tom Cruise.*

"Earlier?" he asked.

"I was the one who hunted down the producer you wanted to talk with, but they only asked me to bring the producer to 'Tom.' NOW I know it was you!" I said, laughing. *Don't be a blondie, Lisa!*

He grinned back, lifted his sunglasses up and looked me straight in the eyes, still shaking my hand, "That was me! It is so nice to meet you." And wow—he really seemed to mean it.

He and Scarlett resumed chatting, so I was able to turn away for a second and tell Aaron what the hold-up was all about.

"She's talking to TOM," I muttered quietly, knowing he would know which Tom I meant. Of course it was Tom Cruise! He was one of the show's hosts that night with Jamie Foxx! *Clueless alert.* Dammit all, I scare myself with how daft I can be at times.

"Well, okay then!" said Aaron. And we left it at that.

Prompter could wait. Producers could wait. The whole freakin' MTV Network would wait if Tom wanted it to.

Can I just say here, that even with all the rumors and weird happenings surrounding Tom Cruise in his career and personal life (and there were some doozies, even back then), I was pleasantly surprised by him? He was engaging, with a smile that ignited the entire crowd. His freaky religious beliefs and antics aside, the fact was he was extremely charismatic (and I'm sure this is what got him where he was in his career, as the Hollywood execs couldn't deny this trait). He made being a magnetic personality look effortless.

This is what I loved about my job. It was so unpredictable, yet so interesting and exciting. I loved every single aspect—the people, the faces, the places. It was all fantastic and I wanted to eat it up.

But it hadn't always been like this. I'd come a very long way from that damaged housewife in Orange County. It wasn't long before this very moment that I'd been a married mother of two who couldn't have dreamed of working for MTV or any other national network. My husband and I had suffered more than our share of setbacks. Among the many things we struggled with, he relapsed into serious intravenous drug abuse after ten years of marriage and twelve years of sobriety. It had been when a fellow sober friend from church, a doctor, prescribed him copious amounts of Oxicontin that things began to unravel. He began popping up to thirty or forty of those babies a day, ending his days of sobriety. He tried to get clean, then turned to street drugs, lost his job, friends and self-respect before finally agreeing to go to rehab for almost a year. After all those trials and more than our fair share of hell, we still decided to move to California to try to make things work.

Now, standing backstage, I felt as though I was being teleported back to that moment three years prior when it all came tumbling down. As I thought about it, I could almost smell the Cling Free on my sheets from that night, when my wonderfully deep sleep was about to be interrupted…

One very late night in Orange County

I rolled over, still half asleep, when I realized someone had come in. *It must be Marcus*, I thought sleepily, with a load of dread and a tinge of fear. I never knew what to expect anymore. We'd been living in separate bedrooms for the last few weeks, while he planned to get settled in his job and find a place of his own. We had come to this agreement because he'd begun using drugs and drinking again and I was not willing to drag the kids through his crap one more time.

Thankfully, Marcus had decided recently that he also didn't want to cause the kids any more pain. I'd been lucky enough to catch him in one of his few lucid moments and get him to agree to move into our little boy's bedroom until he made other arrangements. So far, he'd been pretty good about honoring our agreement.

The last time Marcus went through one of his relapses, we were still living in our home state of New Mexico. He had become hostile and violent at the prospect of our separation and didn't take kindly to being barred from entering his own home. He actually threatened my life in front of one of our dear friends, who was trying to mediate for us. With the calculated plans of a serial killer, he detailed just how easy it would be to murder me. All he had to do, he said, was creep into our room one night and shoot me up with an overdose of cocaine. "Done," he said, proud of what he perceived as brilliance. Our friend called moments after leaving us, in a state of panic saying, "You've got to get out of there, Lisa!" *That was the understatement of the year*, I thought, as I lay there that night recalling the moment in my head.

We'd moved to Orange County because after nine months of rehab, my husband did not want to return to our lives in New Mexico. Even though I wanted to move to Los Angeles to work in television, Marcus did not. He just didn't like the idea of Los Angeles. His therapist backed him up on this, insisting it was too tempting of an environment for him. We settled on Orange County for its beauty and the fond memories we had of traveling through the area.

Fine, I told myself, *I'll get into producing by driving up to L.A. if I need to and Marcus can live and breathe safely in the shelter of Orange County.* I didn't realize at that time that Orange County would not provide a barrier between Marcus and drugs. If he wanted to find and use them, he would. Nor did I realize that moving there would also remove us from our support system—the very people who had helped me extract Marcus from the house and check him into rehab. Despite all conventional wisdom, I still believed that the work had been done in rehab and our lives were off to a fresh, new start.

It was shortly after moving to Orange County that I began to see things differently. Nothing had really changed. Marcus maintained his sobriety for the first few months, but it wasn't long before he was abusing drugs again. I'll never forget the night he came home and was engaged and laughing along with Joel, Graden and me. I thought, *Gee, he's more enthusiastic than usual.* Then I realized he was drunk. He was a happy drunk, and he wasn't complaining about his crappy job, stocking shoes at the sporting goods store, but he was inebriated. According to Marcus, alcohol is what started his downward spiral into drug abuse. My face fell and I immediately left the room and the conversation, putting up a mental wall for the umpteenth time.

I still vividly remember the emotions I felt; the exhaustion and weariness that come from everything revolving around a single person who didn't seem to care about getting better or what he was doing to his family. I remember, either that night or soon after, saying to him with deep resolve and sadness, "I am DONE dealing with all of your problems. I am FINISHED putting my needs aside because my husband has issues! And I am tired of giving!"

Sound selfish? It probably was, but even so, it was that very selfishness that saved my boys and me from further danger and turmoil. A good healthy dose of selfishness can do wonders for your quality of life.

Marcus' disappearing acts soon became the main source of contention. He was supposed to start a new job that day, but he left early in the morning, never called home and it was nearly midnight before I heard his footsteps come up the stairs. I clenched my jaw. Little did I know how much my life was about to change. I felt around in the dark for my little guy, my youngest son, Graden. He was right next to me. We'd been sharing the master bedroom, while his daddy occupied his room.

Wait! Where's Joel? I thought foggily, as I tried to take inventory of the situation. I remembered he went out with friends that night and would be coming home sometime soon. *Poor kid,* I thought. He'd definitely dealt with more than his share during his lifetime. I'd often wished I could wave a magic wand to make his life easier and all things better.

I heard the footsteps stop for a second and then go into the room next door and I breathed a heavy sigh.

As I was finally drifting back to sleep, the bedroom door burst open, the lights flashed on and Marcus stumbled toward my side of the bed. I was immediately wide-awake. After muttering something like, "This is my bedroom," he tried to force his way into bed with us.

Marcus and I wrestled. He squeezed my forearms tight. I'd never felt such pain in my wrists, but this only scared and angered me further. Remarkably, I was able to check on my son through the struggle. *Thank God. Still sleeping,* I kept thinking, as I fought Marcus away.

We said many things in a few seconds, like, "Let go of me! Don't! You agreed! Stop!" And from him, "I don't care! I am sleeping in my bed!" along with a few drunken snickers. As the pressure on my wrists built, so did my fear and anger. I thought *He's a weakling from all the drug abuse and I've worked out my whole life. Get a grip!* And, I was able to push him off me and reach for the telephone.

Sobbing and shaking in my pajamas, I felt very vulnerable, but I was not about to let him take control. He was obviously on drugs, probably crack.

He'd switched to crack a few years earlier because cocaine was so expensive and hard to get. But shooting crack cocaine into one's veins is a very messy business. Literally. Marcus had scars all over his body from the boils his injections caused when they got infected. And it was extremely dangerous to be around someone who used crack. It can make people hostile, even violent. I was afraid. I grabbed the cordless phone and declared, "I'm calling 9-1-1!"

Marcus was easy to predict. I knew that would upset him, so I ran out of the room, luring him after me, then dodged around him and darted back into my bedroom. I slammed the door, locking my little boy and me safe. All the while, my little one slept peacefully in our bed.

Marcus yelled a drugged-out warning, "Lisa! Do NOT call 9-1-1! I'm warning you!" He heard me as I spoke to the operator and I heard him walk into the hall bathroom. Once the call was made, I felt relief. Marcus didn't leave the house and continued to issue warnings that I would regret calling 9-1-1, but I was glad I made the call.

It didn't take long for the flashing lights to illuminate our little gated community and the police to knock on our door. I heard Marcus answer and from my window upstairs, I saw him speaking with the officers. I felt safe as I saw them walk him away from our house and toward the squad car.

Then my older son, Joel, called our house from his friend's car as it drove by.

"Mom, what's going on? There's a bunch of cop cars outside the house!"

Torn apart, I cried as I answered Joel. "Dad's gone a little crazy. You should try to stay at a friend's tonight, because it might not be a good time to come home right now."

I watched from upstairs as Joel and his friends drove away and then I heard another knock on the door. I saw that Marcus was still outside talking with police, so I answered the door.

The police officer standing there was very polite as he asked me to tell my story. I told him how Marcus had stormed in, that we had struggled, but that thankfully I'd been able to push him away to make the call.

He waited for me to finish my story and said, "Well ma'am, we have a slight problem. Your husband says you attacked him." It took just a second for his words to sink in and my jaw to drop to the floor.

"Whaaa? WHAT? Are you kidding me?! What did he say I did?" I demanded.

"He says you dug your nails into him and tried to hurt him… and he *is* bleeding a little." I was flabbergasted. We'd struggled, but *he'd* been the aggressor. It was preposterous to say I had attacked him! This was insanity. And I was baffled at the blood. I had almost no nails, so *where had the blood come from?* I showed the officer my nails and insisted that there was no way in hell my short, peeling, soft, nothing-nails could have inflicted any damage.

"Where is the blood on him?" I asked.

"Well, what he showed us was on the tip of his finger," he stated.

"Oh, come on, Officer!" I pleaded, "Look at these nails! I just had my acrylic nails removed today! Do you really think these could draw blood, much less on the tip of someone's finger?"

"Well, unfortunately, you corroborated his story by saying that you pushed him first," he said matter-of-factly, "So, that makes you the aggressor in the struggle."

"No way!" I said. "You've got to be kidding me!"

"No, ma'am, I'm not. Do you mind if I have a look around the place where the two of you struggled?" he asked. I gladly led him up the stairs, confident there would be no evidence that I was at fault. The officer quietly examined the room and then asked to check out the rest of the upstairs. We walked around and made our way to the hall bathroom my husband had gone into. And there it was: all the evidence the man needed. There was blood smeared all over the mirror and drops of it in the sink. It looked as if someone had been cut and tried to stop the bleeding. I was shocked. I pointed out to the officer that I had no blood on my clothing (a powder-blue, full length cashmere robe, white tee shirt and boxers) and none in my nails, which were down to the quick.

"Well, it looks like there is some color under the nails there," he said.

"That's how everyone's nails are!" I snapped. "I did *not* cut or scratch my husband."

"Well, ma'am," he began, "I'm going to let you in on something. The way the law is and based on the information I have from you and your husband, I would be taking you in and putting you behind bars tonight." I couldn't believe my ears. I was living a real-world nightmare.

"But," he continued, "It's obvious to us that your husband is in no condition to stay here and take care of your son. So, for now, we are not going to do that. I'm going to head outside to talk to him and see if he's willing to stay somewhere else for the night. I'll come back in a few minutes and let you know what we're able to get him to do."

I walked the officer to the door and crumpled onto the couch. *See if he's willing?* I thought. *What just happened?* I was living a full-on Lifetime Original Movie. I was so shocked, I really didn't know what to think or do. A few minutes later the officer came back and told me they'd persuaded Marcus to stay somewhere else for the night. I made one last attempt to convince the officer that I had done nothing to my husband.

"I understand," he said, "And I want to believe you. These are very difficult situations for us to come into and right now, his story has more evidence than yours. I admit, it looks a little suspicious and I admit, I'm probably not seeing the full picture. If you have any other information that might help, feel free to give me a call." As he handed me his card he said, "I'll be working all night."

I was devastated, livid, incredulous and freaking out all at once. I went back up the stairs, growing more outraged with each step. *What in the world had Marcus done now? Did he really think he could frame me for something as incredibly base as this and get away with it? Not today! Not me. He had another thing coming.*

Marcus had just gotten himself into a little war and I was not accustomed to losing. I may have made some wrong turns navigating the waters of the addiction, allowing it to trample our lives, but it wasn't out of weakness or submission on my part. I learned very quickly that trying to control or manipulate the situation was useless. *But stage a coup here in my home, Marcus, then try to turn it on me and say I attacked YOU? And this, by cutting your little finger? Please. If I'd really attacked you, you'd be dead.*

I went back into the hall bathroom to see if I could find any evidence to support my story and there in the waste basket lay my exoneration: a razor blade, dismantled from his razor. He'd obviously used it to cut the tip of his finger, which caused lots of bleeding and created his own little crime scene. *Wow*, I thought, *he really is crazy.*

I went downstairs and plopped down on the living room sofa in shock. How had I not expected something as horrific as this? I had known for months that he was mentally ill. I'd realized that horrible reality with gut-wrenching sobs as he shredded our family back in New Mexico. In a flash I recalled our life then. I remembered pacing the house helplessly, trying to think of someone, *anyone* to talk to… anyone who would understand or relate to my husband's problems or who could help me make sense of the insanity.

I thought about Marcus' addiction at its worst and remembered the burning sting in my throat from crying so much in those long hours, days, weeks and months. How my husband, a born-again assistant pastor by day, a drugged-up zombie by night, started disappearing for days at a time, only to return with his eyes glazed over and wigged out on some unknown drug of the moment. I didn't know a soul I could be balls-out honest with or turn to for real practical help while Marcus hacked away at our family.

I was battling an impossible siege all on my own. Our church friends were so deeply ensconced in their idealistic beliefs about how to handle real-life situations, they were no help to *themselves* let alone me. Besides, Marcus and I were supposed to be examples of how to make wise choices, and of how to live as though every day was a gift. I believed that telling all to some of them would derail even those who were devout in their faith. I recalled with the same burning in my throat, how completely alone I'd felt in this, and yet I was unwilling to be responsible for shattering someone else's faith.

As Marcus began to expose the gravity of his addiction to all those around us, the senior pastors of the church tried to help. They weren't shocked by Marcus' relapse or mental gymnastics, and they tried very hard to be a stabilizing support to us. They met with us (like the time one of them brilliantly suggested "You gotta get outta there!" when Marcus threatened to overdose me), and they came over to protect us when I thought Marcus might try to break in after I changed the locks. But when it came to actually providing real-world solutions, they were crippled. The Bible doesn't specifically address how to deal with drug addicts or how to help the victims, so the church leaders just couldn't figure out what to do for us. And when the church fired Marcus and revoked his ordination, leaving me unable to pay the bills, there was no financial assistance available for Graden, Joel and me—even though I'd seen the church meet other members' financial needs for years before. If I'd been unmarried and destitute through no fault of my own, perhaps they would have helped. But with Marcus choosing his own destruction, the church denied my requests and were hard-pressed to help in any tangible way. They thought they were working wonders by praying for us.

Bless their hearts. It is a grave situation when your survival, peace, stability and endurance depend solely on the success of someone else's prayers. I thought about the Biblical principle of offering your cloak as well if ever asked for your shirt, and wondered how that had been lost when it came to the boys and me. I knew the senior pastors thought Marcus' wealthy family would rescue us, but I'd already asked, and meaningful financial support wasn't coming from them.

I believe that prayer can be powerful and I believe in the incredible force of intention. But I also believe in doing the right thing and in finding and offering real solutions, and our friends showed they were ill prepared over how to do that. To top it off, they made the collective decision not to support me if I chose to divorce Marcus based on his renewed love affair with crack. It's funny how even with signals screaming at you about your unsafe, dysfunctional situation, we humans somehow still find a way to stay.

So, despite everything my instincts told me, I allowed our church's doctrines and beliefs, as well as my mother's advice, to make my decisions for me. Ah yes, my mother. I didn't blame her as I sat there thinking. Not in the least!

My mom and dad had made it through more than forty years of marriage before my dad passed away. Their over-arching belief, which they instilled in all their kids was that you worked things out and you stayed together. Period. And they'd seemed happy and built a pretty great family, so why not?

To be clear, we were not some Norman Rockwell portrait of a perfect family. As we kids grew up and started to rebel, the cracks were exposed. My mother either thought that men could do no wrong, or she held a deeply rooted Catholic belief that if they did, as a woman, you bit your tongue and dealt with it. She also somehow developed the notion that women are strong, and can and should fix everything. Come to think of it, maybe she *really* believed men were clueless and wouldn't survive without a woman's help. Huh.

Either way, this meant that no matter what, she would stay married, and no matter what, even after our dad died, she would support, help and fix all the problems she could for her sons—to their detriment, I believe. Even as kids, when my brothers behaved atrociously or were at times cruel, verbally abusive or disrespectful to their siblings, pets, belongings and to her, my mother stood by their side, defending them and doing what she could to fix things.

As I sat on my sofa looking back on all of this, believe it or not, I still remembered most of my childhood experiences fondly. The good times and the funny memories growing up as a little girl in our neighborhood were pretty awesome. I got my whacky sense of humor from hanging with my brothers and my now-departed sister Mimi, who at six years my senior was the sister closest in age to me. My other sisters were gone and out of the home as I grew up.

I had positive recollections because my brothers weren't horrible *all* of the time. Most times we laughed, played games like kick-ball or flag-football, watched television or hung out together and enjoyed life. But despite the good times, it only took a few insane instances to teach me to stay out of their way when these moments arose. God knows I was well aware of what they were capable of. Like the night we were left with a pitiful, unsuspecting sitter and the boys chased each other around with giant kitchen knives, and I was sure one of them would die; or the time they decided to find out what would happen if they swung our family cat around by the tail. I knew I didn't want to be around for their *Lord of the Flies* reenactment.

As I sat there on my reflection couch in the OC, I came to the conclusion that my father's presence had much to do with any stability we kids felt around us growing up. When the boys were brutal or hard to be around, dad was always there with a strong hand (or back-hand…or belt, to be exact) to keep things in order. I learned early on to proactively defend myself from the hurtful words or bullying antics of my brothers. My sister Mimi lovingly gave me the nickname of Wonder Brat in my young twenties (again, all in love and jest), because I simply wouldn't take anyone's shit, and that part of me came from those lessons learned in the trenches with my brothers. To me it was a badge of honor. I was proud to think I could stand tall against any male figure that would dare try to take me down. But our poor mom was left to deal with everything on her own, the only way she knew how when our dad, a long-term smoker, died at sixty-five of cancer and emphysema.

I wasn't sitting there analyzing it all, really. I was simply reflecting as I often do. My mom was a loving, beautiful, tender person, and she made each of us kids feel as though we were her favorite, even though her judgment about the boys was skewed. All I could figure was that she leaned heavily toward thinking the boys were always right and could do no wrong. It seemed as though the idea was almost *sacred* to her. There was *no* discussing it, ever. I realized as I sat there thinking, it was probably this, coupled with my own personally developed self-defense mechanism toward my brothers, which helped me form my own opinions about males in general. I decided that just because a guy liked or approved of something, did not mean it was right. I chose not to believe men had the answers to life, could do no wrong, or held some magic key to my happiness.

I realized sadly that this belief I was so proud of hadn't influenced my judgments or choices when I began to date—certainly not when I met Marcus. No, my mother's beautiful tenderness toward all in her life was something to cherish. I wanted *that* to be my hallmark, not bitter, defensive, skeptical bitchiness. So finding the appropriate situations in which to express that same tenderness became a challenge—the kind you never really master. I vacillated between extremes of strong independence and being a tender caretaker or fixer for much of my life, and I had veered more toward fixer when I met and married Marcus. Just because I had married Marcus, my views about men and my strong sense of self hadn't eroded completely. But people learn best from their own mistakes, and boy, had I made them!

Even with my life-taught views of men, and as horrific as things got with Marcus after we'd moved to Orange County, and even after he started drinking and using drugs again, I somehow thought keeping my own little family together was still the primary goal. I still thought we could "work it out."

I know. As my grandmother, Umanita Tamoroglio would say, "IDIOTA!" or, BLONDIE!

But try to frame me for attacking you, Marcus…or put my ability to care for my sons in jeopardy, then guess what? I'm done. FINALLY. But now that you've done it…this STUPID, IDIOTIC move, you're going to see what I'm capable of, and you're not going to like it. This is where this ENDS.

I got up from the couch, picked up the phone and dialed the number on the police officer's card. I caught him at his desk and told him that, after doing a little investigation of my own, I'd found something he might be interested in.

"It sounds very possible that he could have used a razor," the officer agreed. "We aren't going to file any charges here tonight, so this case will remain open. Let us know if you need anything else."

I breathed a heavy sigh of relief, though I knew my battle was just beginning. I counted myself lucky throughout the entire ordeal. Even though the surreal nightmare was like a bad movie, I'd gotten out virtually unscathed (physically) and neither of my sons had seen all that really happened that night.

As I stood under the boom mic watching Tom Cruise and Scarlett Johansson jokingly compare bicep sizes, I smiled. *No. She couldn't possibly have any idea of where I've been.*

Scarlett and I finally made it onto the soundstage, where I led her to prompter and I sighed aloud as I recalled the moment when Marcus finally told me he planned to move permanently back to New Mexico to be with his family. Oh, the relief I'd felt! When he told me this, the boys and I had just returned to Orange County from a disastrous trip to Albuquerque for the holidays. It had only been a few weeks since the 9-1-1 telephone call *incident*. Believe it or not, Marcus had somehow negotiated himself back into our home until he could get on his feet, while we supposedly planned for divorce. Even then, I began to see the fruits of my *not* telling the boys all that was going on with Marcus.

But I had no idea how to tell a four-year-old boy his daddy preferred the high of crack cocaine to that of being a happy part of our family, nor did I ever think I should. Joel knew there were issues, but tried not to know too much. All Graden knew was that daddy was sick. This only perpetuated his desire to snuggle and help his daddy as much as he could. My determination to make Marcus pay for framing me and threatening the safety of the boys, my resolve to get things back on track for myself and to eradicate this insanity from our lives, had been suffocated by the sweet adoration that Graden felt for his daddy. In those couple of weeks, things were nowhere near peaceful, but we managed. We drove to Albuquerque together and Marcus immediately began disappearing. He'd finally materialized on Christmas morning at his brother's house, drugged up. He sat there after opening his gifts and informed me that he planned to stay in Albuquerque and keep Graden with him while *I worked on MY issues.*

I stole away in the middle of the night back to Orange County, leaving Marcus behind. I never looked back.

I felt so relieved that he didn't plan to return to California. I remembered the bliss I felt as I thought of finally being able to pick up the pieces, to make my own choices about my life and to try to rebuild in peace.

It was the safe and final separation and impending divorce from Marcus that empowered and emancipated me, enabling me to finally do things for the boys and myself. Joel, who'd been in therapy since Marcus's first relapse, retold the entire 9-1-1 episode to his therapist. By law, she was required to report it to social services. As awful as that may sound, it turned out to be a blessing, as the state then offered to pay for therapy for all three of us.

Social services became my new support system and ally. They saw what had been really going on and were satisfied to see that the real danger, Marcus, no longer lived in the house. Little did I know of the awesome, incredible adventure of a lifetime I was about to embark on as a result of making it through to the other side of the pain.

Mommy Needs A Makeover

*"Is the cheese on the omelet shredded or sliced?
If it's shredded, I'd like a teaspoon.
If it's sliced, can you ask them to only use a quarter slice?"*

It was January; 2001. I was walking into a new chapter, all on my own. Marcus had been gone for about a month and that situation seemed quiet for now. It did worry me a little once I fully realized where my life had taken me, and the level I had allowed things to sink to. Starting over on my own was daunting. How ill-prepared I was to be self-supporting again! I was thirty-five. My long-sought college degree was still being sought when I had spare time. I'd been trying my hand at professional acting and working toward a career in the film and television industry, something I'd always dreamed of, more often than working in a job that paid the bills. Life with Marcus had provided a steady dividend from his family's rental properties—not enough to pay all the bills, but something to count on.

A quick personal inventory revealed that the only way I was going to survive was to take charge and forge ahead in a new direction.

Forging ahead was no small task. As much as I longed for my family to cling together during this difficult time, my older son, Joel, who was sixteen, was dealing with some demons of his own. We grappled with some regular teenage rebellion issues along the way, but even more significant incidents happened after my final separation from Marcus. Joel painted his bedroom and his fingernails black—a habit he'd developed after his first girlfriend painted his nails black in Albuquerque, started wearing eyeliner and dressed in ripped, dark clothes.

I wasn't an idiot. I knew it was that trendy, spooky kind of serial killer, I mean *"Goth"* look. I'd sort of accepted all of that already. But when he started coming home very late, or not at all, without calling, the real arguments began. In spite of all the time Joel spent seeing a therapist, he continued to grow more distant and less responsive to authority of any kind, especially mine.

Great. He's blaming me for this shit of a mess, I thought, bewildered. I was at my wit's end trying to figure out ways to work with Joel and to live peaceably. I succumbed to every suggestion and answered every probing question his therapist asked of me. I stopped visiting friends up in Los Angeles. I cleared my schedule to be free to hang out with my boys. I took a real interest in Joel's interests: his favorite poets, music, artists and more. I tried to get to know his friends and welcomed them into our home, all to no avail. I even tried to sit there with a straight face at the therapist's asinine, whacked-out insinuation that Joel's father (not Marcus) abused me while I was pregnant with Joel. She surmised all of this from the "drawings Joel made in the sand." She explained in complete seriousness that it probably was the reason for Joel's issues, even though I insisted that I'd only seen Joel's dad while pregnant once, in public, and he never laid a hand on me.

What is it about me that attracts these whack-hammers into my life? How the hell did we find THIS therapist, of all the thousands available in Orange County? My controlled and emphatic "No," only made her insist further.

"Even if Joel were to say now that he fabricated these drawings on purpose, it is highly probable you really were abused and his drawings are very real images coming from his subconscious mind and as such, are still very telling," she said. She was basically, in her condescending way, accusing me of lying.

If what she said were even *close* to any possible reality, I may have seen her "diagnosis" as enlightened, even life-saving. But this woman had no idea of whom she was speaking. She didn't know that at the age of 18 I'd made the decision *not* to marry Joel's father. I'd been working toward going away to college. Though I was dating Joel's dad, I was looking forward to moving away to school and getting on with my life. But then the morning sickness kicked in and everything changed. When Joel's dad expressed disgust at me over the phone for becoming pregnant (because we *all* know I did it alone) and suggested that we marry as quickly as possible so he could get the tax write-off, I chose to sever all ties with him. Those were some painful months living at home with my very Catholic mother and my happy-go-lucky dad. It was not easy asking my dad to answer the repeated phone calls and hearing him tell the guy to quit calling. I didn't want to hurt Joel's dad, but I had a very different vision of my life than what he could imagine. I'd seen more than one of my four sisters marry out of *necessity*, only to have the marriages end after too many lost years and way too much pain.

I never would have agreed to even *see* Joel's dad while I was pregnant, but my dad actually felt sorry for the guy and suggested I at least meet him in person to break things off. I was smart enough to realize how uncommon this concession was, considering I was my dad's baby girl. This gesture won my dad heaps of respect as I grew older.

I agreed to meet Joel's dad in the parking lot of the Mr. Donut, where I broke things off with finality. Joel's dad cried. It was one of the hardest things I've ever done. It wasn't until Joel was six months old, started to crawl and do so many adorably cute baby things, that I thought his dad might want to (and probably should) be involved in his life. We arranged a meeting at a public park in Albuquerque and their relationship began.

So, who the hell did this whack-job therapist think she was? The fact that I had no credibility with her infuriated me. I found it abusive, and the abuse came at the *wrong* time. She was about to find out what happens when you push a victim of mental and verbal abuse too far. When she finally stopped yapping, I reached across her little woo-woo sandbox sitting area and slapped the shit out of her.

Okay, I *wish* I had. Oh how satisfying that would have been! Instead, I fired her on the spot. I should have reported her.

I knew that Joel was obviously hurting and unable to express his thoughts and feelings through words. He was either trying to show the world how angry he was, or he desperately wanted to find peace in his own way, and was willing to disrupt everything to do so. But there finally came a time when his behavior eclipsed my tolerance level and I was forced to lay down the law. I gave him the option of either abiding by my household rules or moving back to New Mexico to live with his biological father. Marcus even tried from a distance to support me in all of it.

But Joel defied everything, including our final warnings, by choosing to move in with the parents of a good friend who'd opened their home to him.

I was heartbroken. *Now what?* The truth was, Joel did blame me, as he always had. I was the one who'd always been there, so I think I was the only one he felt he could safely blame. It didn't make it right, but it was our reality.

The night Joel said he was moving to his friend's house, my survival instinct kicked in and I instantly went numb. In hindsight, I realize that numbness enabled me to make rational decisions. The pain over allowing my son to move in with some other parents would come later, but right then I was not affected by my emotions. As I spoke to Joel about his desire to live with his friend's parents, I was calm.

"You realize if you do this, you are choosing to live on your own, without any financial support from Marcus or me?" I asked.

"Yes." he said blankly.

"How are you going to finish school?" I prodded.

"The same way I have been," he retorted. Joel had not enjoyed high school in his freshman year; he and I had agreed that if he tried it and hated it, I would home-school him. At first I was extremely involved, overseeing his studies in literature, languages, the arts and phys-ed, as well as the basics. Then we discovered a correspondence school that interacted with the students, handling exams, homework and everything via snail mail—you know, the good ole' US Mail.

"Okay," I said, "I hope you don't give that up. It's important." It was a difficult decision. I went upstairs and took a long, sad look around his room; at the music collection he'd built over the years, the posters of musicians he idolized, the guitars that surrounded his furniture. I would miss him so much, yet he had no idea. But I had to let him get through his pain somehow and I was all out of solutions.

In the weeks that followed, I came to the startling realization that my husband had left me (for which I was thankful), my older son was making a beeline for the door, and now my own dreams and even self-esteem had left me.

But my five-year-old son desperately needed me to be strong and happy.

I spent the first few weeks after Joel moved out floundering around like a fish out of water, somewhat in a daze. I wasn't sure where to begin.

The biggest shock to me was the loss of our family's entire infrastructure. There was no *team* to work toward common goals. There was no *partner* to smile or cry with as our kids grew and made mistakes. There was only me, hurting as I saw my sons struggling to understand. I also wondered if I would ever be wanted by anyone else. Thoughts like "Will I ever be able to find another person to spend my days on earth with?" consumed me. It was unnerving. After the years of mental, verbal and personal abuse, I felt undesirable. I was too heavy, at least by my standards, never having lost the "baby weight" from my younger son to attract *anyone*. But when my daze started to clear, I began to get a sense of the ME that I knew was somewhere underneath it all, and I determined this: the negative, fearful thinking, and anything that kept me floundering was unacceptable.

Oy, what a mess! I thought. *It's time to clean house and get some things in order.*

I realized I could only successfully attack one problem at a time. I decided that my first priority had to be to take care of me. ME ME ME

ME ME! I needed to shed some pounds. It was time to lose the slightly dumpy housewife look. Losing weight and getting in shape would satisfy and empower me, which in turn would encourage and energize me to be a positive help to Graden. Feeling good about myself became imperative.

Every *other* time I'd faced dilemmas with my kids or my home life, I'd been selfless and sacrificing, to my own neglect. But this… THIS was going to be different. "Well-adjusted mommy equals well-adjusted kids," became my mantra. Besides, I was the queen of multitasking and this was an optimum example of killing several birds with one stone.

I was suddenly energized, with an inkling of a sense of direction in mind (just an *inkling of a sense*). One look in my closet revealed a host of frumpy frocks only there to accommodate extra body fat. All of the cool, trendy clothes that fit me pre-baby were so dated they *almost* qualified as retro. Perusing my wardrobe, *ah, the five-inch-thick shoulder pad phase, uh huh*, plunged me into memories of dancing to the *Pet Shop Boys* at the trendiest nightclubs in town. I thought of my gorgeous girlfriends and me with our big, long, curly manes, strutting our stuff, not caring whether any men asked us to dance. We would dance all night together. Having fun was all that mattered. We thought we were something else in our Karen Alexander dresses, Esprit tops, Z Cavaricci jeans and Benetton threads. It was funny to recall those images as I looked at some of the clothes now hanging in my closet, wondering what in the world I, or the fashion world for that matter, was thinking back then.

I continued on. Hanging next to the pre-baby stuff was an entire wardrobe I didn't like, in small, medium, and large variations, just in case I put on or lost a few pounds. *Why did I buy so many Units pieces?* I thought, laughing now. Units were all the rage for a very short time, for a reason. They were separate pieces of stretchy, lycra-style fabric that you could mix and match to create a whole wardrobe. I was disgusted. If I had to look at one more pair of dowdy, stretchy pants, mixy-matchy tops, sashes, or stretch socks, I was going to hurl.

I realized I needed to make some changes and fast. *I will never put pounds on again,* I promised myself. Losing weight was now a requirement.

If I were going to be happy again, I knew I would have to take charge of my body and never let the real me get lost again.

I tossed every nonessential, nonsensical piece of clothing. If I didn't like it or it was large (and couldn't easily be taken in), off to charity it went. I think I whittled it all down to about eight or ten complete outfits that could safely stay in my wardrobe. I kept only what I desperately needed for work.

Work! I would have to do that again, wouldn't I? Get a real job. I'd been working from home on a *very* part-time basis, consulting in marketing and public relations, but it wasn't enough to pay the bills.

The thought of bills made me sick. Just that morning, I had opened my credit card statement to discover a thousand-dollar charge from a strip club. Did my ex really think I was going to pay for his lap dances at a strip bar?

You can handle it, Lisa! Just remember how great it feels to be free! I was so glad to be rid of him at that point, I convinced myself the charge was a bargain. I had to. In my mind it was either buck up and get stronger, or curl up into a ball and whither away.

So what now? What about *my* dreams of working in television and film, of writing and producing? I made the decision any responsible mother would. I quickly found a good-paying job with incredible benefits at a large corporation close to home. I was hired to put my marketing and research capabilities to work on a global scale at an engineering firm that spanned over twenty countries, worldwide. Okay, I was hired as a marketing assistant. But it was a great start!

I also signed up for the neighborhood weight loss program and attended faithfully. I followed that program like the Moonies drank the Kool-Aid (I may be mixing cults here).

Sample of my daily weight-loss routine

6:00 AM	Wake up. Get ready for work. Ignore hunger pangs, if any. They are the enemy.
7:00 AM	Make breakfast: Egg whites with grilled vegetables, dry toast with low-fat butter-flavored spread, decaffeinated coffee, no cream.
7:45 AM	Take son to school; go to work.
9:30 AM	If hunger pangs come back, drink more decaf. DO NOT eat snack until at least 10:30 AM.
10:29 AM	Watch clock. Get ready to eat snack.
10:30 AM	Devour snack: tiny apple or baby banana. If still hungry, eat ten peeled baby carrots.
11:30 AM	Drink water. Lots of water. Drink a diet, caffeine-free soda to fool hunger pangs (the enemy).
11:55 AM	Microwave low-calorie packaged dinner.
12:00 noon	Enjoy that sumptuous microwaved meal of the day, consisting of something like rigatoni with chicken and broccoli. If still hungry, heat an entire can of green beans in microwave. Add salt and pepper. Enjoy! Apparently I could live in a trailer park, because I actually *do* enjoy canned green beans. I'm an anomaly.
3:00 PM	Eat more carrots. Drink water, herbal tea or have another caffeine-free diet beverage or decaf coffee.
5:30 PM	Pick up son from after-school care. Cook dinner: grilled or steamed vegetables (no oil or butter),

	grilled, skinless, boneless chicken breast. No butter, cream or fattening sauce.
6:30 PM	Dessert: yogurt and more carrots. Perhaps enjoy a low-calorie popcorn or sugar-free pudding.
8:00 PM	Ignore hunger pangs (they are the enemy). If all else fails, go to bed.

Before anyone gets their panties in a bunch, here's a little more info: As much as it appears to be some twisted sort of starvation diet, it is not. Believe it or not, it is a doctor-approved, well-balanced, nutritious diet—except for the "filler" items I inserted, like diet beverages and coffee.

I tell ya, when I stick to something, like, a *realistic* diet that fits my lifestyle, I see great results quickly. I remember the ladies in my little neighborhood telling me about their "concern over my weight loss"—even though I was losing an average of a pound a week, which is healthy and safe. These ladies were *worried*. Did I mention they were overweight and unhappy themselves? It's funny how that works. I knew they were projecting onto me the same excuses they used for themselves whenever they tried to diet. But I maintained a "whatever" mentality. All I knew was I was succeeding and I felt great, energetic, and healthier than ever.

Awesome, right? I know. Blah-blah-blah! It actually kind of *sucked* in the beginning, because I was depriving my body of my normal course of lard (yum), sugar (yum) and baked goods (delish) I had been eating for years. I *chose* to view the hunger pangs as the enemy in order to get past them and allow my stomach to shrink a little and my body to catch up with the change in my lifestyle. At times, I found that napping or going to bed early, especially on the weekends, when I was home all day, helped a lot. As time went on and I became used to my new regimen, I was able to enjoy occasional meals out at restaurants. I knew the places to avoid, but I became an expert at staying on my diet no matter what was on that menu. I remember cracking up or embarrassing my friends with my *When Harry Met Sally* style of ordering food (if you don't know of the zany way Sally, played by Meg Ryan, ordered food, you must watch the movie!). "Do you have low-fat cottage cheese? No? How about *Smart Balance* spread instead of butter? The kind with olive oil?" I believe in finding a way to maintain a healthy diet no matter where I dine.

Now, I was not just religious about my diet; I was extreme and dogmatic. No one or thing was going to keep me from getting back to the "me" that I had once been.

At times, when I thought I might pass out from exhaustion or burst into tears from stress, I thought of my mom. She had mothered *eleven* kids. She'd birthed more, but not all survived. She was the Eveready Bunny of mothers who worked. Yep, my mom worked. This was huge when I was growing up in the late sixties and early seventies. She and my dad operated a very successful business. With demanding schedules and unruly kids wreaking havoc on the neighborhood, my mom was still the most beautiful, together mother on the block, maybe even in the whole community where we lived. Even into her eighties, she was one of the most beautiful ladies most people had ever known. Her personality attracted like a magnet.

Mom as a young wife.

Me as a toddler with my mom, in our backyard.

Mom as I remember her (at work at the printing plant) from when I was a kid growing up.

One night, after working a very long day, I came home to find my younger son Graden crying. He was upset about something, but couldn't articulate why. I knew he needed me. He needed to snuggle and be held, but I was so tired. I took him upstairs and tucked us both into my bed without even getting undressed. I lay there in the dark, crying silently. I cried over the loss of childhood both of my boys were suffering, I cried because I didn't know how I was going to recover from the strip-club debt my husband left me, I cried from loneliness as well. I was no longer "with" someone and though that was a good thing in the long run, I felt very lonely.

And the loneliness was nothing. It had been so long since I'd enjoyed *sex* and felt sexy, I wasn't sure I would recognize sexual arousal if it hit me between the eyes (I know... I'm mixing my metaphors here). Should my hormones rise up and bite me in the face, I felt sure I would keel over, not knowing what bit me. As I lay there weeping, almost uncontrollably, I realized I was drifting into sleep from sheer exhaustion.

All of these difficult times confirmed for me how critical my need was to talk to someone. Therapy, in my mind, was essential for both Graden and me. We desperately needed someone to talk to, someone who knew what the heck they were talking about. If we didn't, I knew I was destined to be a bicycle helmet-wearing loon with Graden circling me, mumbling. It was going to be good to do some important inner work while everything on the outside was unraveling. I'd allowed my own self to slip through my fingers over the years, and I was determined, in spite of all the pain around me and inside of me, to reach back and remember who I used to be. I planned to do whatever I must in order to deal with any of my "issues" as soon as I became aware of them. And I did not want to repeat the relationship mistakes I'd made in the past.

So enter therapy my little boy and I did, and it was the best gift we ever gave ourselves. The first thing I did with my therapist was set some goals:

1) Realize my own value.
2) Forget about making more friends or *pursuing* the ones I had (something I had always done); let them do that.

3) Approach life and relationships in a whole new way.

These were lofty goals, but I was ready to do the work involved. One of the best things I took away from my very intuitive therapist, something that has been an important, consistent reminder to me ever since, was a little work of prose she gave me to put on my refrigerator:

Your Audience is Important

Life is a Theatre—Invite Your Audience Carefully.

Not everyone is healthy enough to have a front row seat in our lives. There are some people in your life that need to be loved from a distance.

It's amazing what you can accomplish when you let go of, or at least minimize your time with draining, negative, incompatible, not-going-anywhere relationships and friendships.

Observe the relationships around you. Pay attention. Which ones lift and which ones lean? Which ones encourage and which ones discourage? Which ones are on a path of growth uphill and which ones are going downhill?

When you leave certain people, do you feel better or feel worse?

Which ones always have drama or don't really understand, know or appreciate you?

The more you seek quality, respect, growth, peace of mind, love and truth around you, the easier it will become for you to decide who gets to sit in the front row and who should be moved to the balcony of your life.

If you cannot "change" the people around you, change the people you're around.

—Author Unknown

After that, whenever I felt I was at the end of my rope, I learned to look myself in the mirror and give myself a good talking to. "Get a grip, Lisa." I would say. "You are an intelligent, energetic, vivacious woman, who has so much to offer this planet." I'm not sure how I stumbled on this handy little tactic, but believe it or not, pep talks like that strengthened and encouraged me. It was great therapy! "You are NOT going to let this beat you! You are a winner! You succeed at whatever you put your mind to! You are beautiful! You are thin!" Whatever the issue was that day, I would do battle over it in front of the mirror. There was no room for failure. I would not allow hurtful memories or doubtful feelings to bring me down. I would think about them, work through them, and move on. I also determined I was not going to waste any more time with people who weren't also successful, motivated and inspirational.

My nuclear family spent the initial phase of the separation and divorce in serious repair mode. My little boy took his cues from me: how I felt about and responded to the life around us affected him immensely. As I began to shape up inside and out, he was calmed and became adjusted to our new life.

But what about my new job? My palms became clammy every time I thought about my big first day back to work. Just about everything in my life was uncertain as I pulled into the giant parking lot to start my first day. This job held tremendous promise for me, but I wasn't sure how I would fit into the corporate world. I wasn't sure how I would handle the juggling act as a single mom again either, but I found I thrived on the adult interaction. I laughed with coworkers at non-knock-knock jokes, and listened to intelligent people as we collaborated on projects. And thank GOD, not a single *one* of them were blitzed or freaking out from drug use! Amazing!

As I lost weight and my wardrobe gradually improved, I started gaining attention from men, as well as kudos and compliments from female friends at the office. This was like frosting on a well-deserved cake – the kind you know is coming on your birthday, so you diet and abstain from every kind of yummy food or drink, knowing you can indulge later. By *god* I loved that cake. Of course, I got true joy from loving and caring for both of my boys, but *this,* the positive attention from other adults, gave me my happy dance back. It also made me feel validated as a human being.

One gorgeous chick at the office modeled the essential cool of the corporate world for me. She had a short, spunky and up-to-date hairstyle and seemed to be able to combine that sunny Southern California look with what seemed appropriate for Corporate America. I found the hair stylist I see to this day through her.

All of these things energized me and enabled me to go home at night and give all my attention to Graden. After work and school each day, we loved hanging out in front with all of the neighbors and their kids. The kids would ride their bikes up and down our street, while the moms and some of the dads would visit and catch up. Though I realized my sons and I were still like shattered pieces of glass and were trying hard to *find* all the pieces, let alone put them back together, we were also off to the start of our new lives. So far, it felt pretty good.

Bring Me A Mint Julep

*"Oh, give me the beat, boys and free my soul,
I want to get lost in your rock and roll and drift away."*
—Mentor Williams

After months of intense physical and emotional work following Marcus' departure, I started to like how I felt and what I saw in the mirror. I was happy with the path I had taken. I was all on my own again, but I was beginning to smile and enjoy life.

In May, Brittany, one of my best girlfriends (a television personality for *E! Entertainment Television* in L.A. at the time), invited me to be her guest at the Mint Jubilee in Louisville, Kentucky, which she was hosting that year. She knew of my aspirations of working in television as well as the nightmare rollercoaster I'd just gotten off. She extended the invitation in part to give me a nice reprieve, but also to introduce me to her world.

The Mint Jubilee was a televised charitable event on the eve of the Kentucky Derby. "I am considered 'talent' because I'm hosting the show, which also means I am allowed to bring a guest along!" she announced, excited. "And guess what?"

"What?" I asked.

"We get to fly first class." She knew this would be special for me, though it was old hat to her. She was accustomed to flying first class, staying at the finest hotels and receiving celebrity treatment. It was part of the gig, at least back in the days of immense industry budgets. I refer to those days as the "high times" for the entertainment industry. Ah, the good ole days.

"This *is* a charitable event," she forewarned me, "So I am not sure what our hotel arrangements will be. Everyone who is involved is doing it pro-bono. None of us is paid, but hotel, food, and drinks will be taken care of. They also have airline and car sponsors, so the main things are covered. We even get our own sheriff!"

I looked at her. "Sheriff? Why do we 'get' our own sheriff?"

"Well, assassination attempts are pretty common in the South. They apparently *hate* celebrities," she said.

Wait…what? I give her credit, because she kept a straight face for about five seconds before she broke up in laughter. "No, the charity gets the assistance of the Sheriff's Department for security, mainly because of the talent and the celebrities who come in for the weekend."

"Wow. It's a really big deal, then."

"Yep," she confirmed, excitedly. "I hope we get the same sheriff I had last year. I requested him. I called him Sheriff Bob. It's so cute. They are all so polite and have such great southern manners. Everything is 'yes, ma'am, no ma'am'… and they open the doors for you everywhere. It's really great! If we get him, he'll be the one to pick us up at the airport."

This weekend was going to be memorable and I felt privileged to be included. *Boy, do I need this*, I thought with a heavy, relieved sigh. I was so glad that my sister and mother were able to fly out from New Mexico for a little vacation and take care of Graden! I felt pretty lucky.

Though the last few months (not to mention years) had been tough, I felt like my life was finally going in the right direction for a change—a direction that *I* chose, thank you very much. I even told Britt on the flight to Kentucky just how happy I was at my new job with its incredible benefits, college degree program and everything else it had to offer. I was fairly emphatic, come to think of it. Little did she or I know the fire the upcoming weekend would light under me, or how it would derail, in a good way, any corporate aspirations I'd entertained.

When we arrived at Louisville's Standiford Field Airport, Sheriff Bob was at the gate. He whisked us over to baggage claim, picked up our bags and led us to his SUV in front of the terminal. It was everything Britt had said. I felt like a celebrity myself and it was pretty friggin' fantastic. As we drove to the hotel for "talent check-in," I took a good look around Louisville. I'd never been to the city, which lies at the falls of the Ohio River. It was full of character and beauty, with interesting architecture.

When we arrived at the historic Brown Hotel, the talent manager asked us to attend a production meeting that was in progress in the hospitality suite. We picked up our all-access credentials and made our way upstairs. As we threw our bags into our suite and walked over to the meeting, my excitement and anticipation grew. I'd worked on production crews for network-affiliate nightly news back in New Mexico. I realized then that I wanted to write and produce for film or television. It was what I wanted to do with my life. I just wasn't sure back then which of the two, or how to go about it; then the mess with Marcus pulled my attention and focus and brought pursuing the dream to a screeching halt. Now, I was thrilled at the chance to be a fly on the wall in this production meeting and Britt, my biggest supporter, was happy to include me.

A group of guys invented and ran the Mint Jubilee. One of them was television actor Matt Battaglia, who was known (back then) for his work on several popular shows of the day including *Friends*, *That'70s Show*, and more recently, *NCIS: Los Angeles, CSI: NY,* and others. He and his buddies, the Theineman brothers, were from the Louisville, Kentucky area originally. The Mint Jubilee was an event benefiting cancer research, a cause that was special to Matt because his mother died of cancer. Though Matt wasn't in that production meeting, I met his assistant and the rest of the crew.

It was immediately obvious to me what an incredibly creative, vibrant group this was. They were all professional television industry folks from Los Angeles who worked with MTV, VH-1 and every other major network producing music television specials. There was one guy in particular who caught my eye. I remember thinking, *Hello, Gorgeous!* He looked like a cross between Johnny Depp and a young Antonio Banderas. His hair was just long enough to touch his shoulders, and he had these deep, dark Latin eyes that seemed to penetrate. He sported a goatee, which in another lifetime may have repelled me, but he rocked that thing. He was the show's stage manager and as I listened to everyone debate how to organize the show, I realized this business was not for idiots or people who did not know what they were doing.

Aaron Anderson, the show's producer, greeted Britt and me warmly and gave us a quick rundown. We discussed Britt's hair, makeup and wardrobe, as well as the rehearsal and event schedule.

Once the wardrobe was decided, Britt and I were whisked off to the convention center for a tour of the venue as well as a brief run-through of the introductions she would make. Some very well-known celebrities were flying in for the events, and we were about to mingle and party with them all. I watched Britt expertly run through the rehearsal and was so proud to see how far she'd come. Britt bent over backwards to make me feel welcomed and believed in, but somehow I still felt somewhat like a child looking longingly at the adorable puppy in the pet shop window. I instantly wanted this life, but felt like a fish out of water and naked as a newly divorced woman. I was sure everyone had gotten the memo on me, and could see only a frail little thing before them.

I know. *WHAT?* Seriously, Britt and I both had come a long way since our days as young up-and-comers in New Mexico, but our paths had gone in two completely different directions. Though I was not working in television or another arena that inspired me creatively at the time, I was being pulled back toward my dream and began to wonder if maybe my time would still come.

After the rehearsal, we rushed back to the hotel to get ready for the first mixer and of course the conversation turned to important business: the cute guys. Britt was single as well and had a little history with this group of friends.

"Have you seen anyone you think is cute or has potential?" she asked, prodding me for the 4-1-1.

"Pffffhhh!" I huffed, sarcastically. "Well, yeah!" I added. "You didn't tell me about the gorgeous guys! That guy Antonio is pretty hot!" referring to the stage manager at the production meeting.

"Ahhhhaaa!" she said knowingly, "Good choice. I think he is, too! You should definitely go for him!" she said. *Go for him?* I hadn't even *thought* of "going for" *anyone* on this trip. It hadn't even crossed my mind.

Until now.

"You know, I dated Brian after last year's Jubilee, and he was being very friendly in there. I definitely felt some chemistry," she continued happily, "It'll be interesting to see what happens this weekend."

Once we were primped and ready to go, we made our way to one of Louisville's hottest restaurants, one with some fabulous name like "The Blue Door" or "Chelsea" or something, where we had the run of the place for our private party. The atmosphere was very trendy and cool, the food and drinks fabulous, and the company amazing.

It was the first night of the long weekend, and several of the A-list celebrities had not yet arrived. These included Chloe Sevigny, known from her role in *Boys Don't Cry* and more recently for *Big Love* on HBO; Thora Birch from *American Beauty*; Melissa Joan Hart from *Sabrina the Teenage Witch*; Sean Young from films like *Ace Ventura: Pet Detective*; Wendy Malick from *Just Shoot Me* and most recently known for her role in *Hot in Cleveland*; Shannon Elizabeth from *American Pie,* and its sequels; Dana Delaney, known best then for her role in *China Beach* and the movie *Tombstone* but more recently for *Body of Proof* and a short run on *Desperate Housewives.* Many others would be making an appearance as well.

One couple had arrived: French Stewart, known then for his quirky role on *Third Rock from the Sun* and his then-wife Katherine La Nasa, from another show at the time, *Three Sisters*. They invited us to join them at their table for a drink. French, it turned out, had grown up in New Mexico, and we laughed when we found out he and I had lived near each other. He cracked us up talking about the Albuquerque hangouts, like 4B's restaurant.

After that, Britt and I meandered a little and landed at a table with some young, hot guys. All her friends and acquaintances, it seemed, were young and hot. We joked, laughed and flirted. One of the guys was senior legal counsel at Miramax, while another was a studio musician; a third was none other than hottie Antonio.

It felt amazing to be showered with so much positive attention. These people were living their dreams and loving life! It was inspiring and attractive and I wanted more. I had a voracious appetite for life and wanted to devour every tasty morsel in sight. There was no stopping me. I felt pretty good this evening, dressed in some black leather capri pants and a bright sleeveless top. Trust me. It was all the rage then. My hair, recently cut and streaked in my cute short 'do, was the talk of the publicists and stylists in town from Los Angeles—they literally pulled me into a room and wanted to lift the hair up to see how it was cut, and asked me specifically where I had it done. I realized then that dressing for this weekend in anything other than trendy or hot was out of the question. Good thing that, like the Boy Scouts, I was *always* prepared. It was absolutely crucial to dress to the nines for every single event and take no prisoners in the process. As I calculated these decisions, I realized I was up to something. *What?* Apparently to catch myself a hot Latin guy named Antonio for the weekend (insert evil laugh).

Britt & I ready for a night out in Louisville, KY, 2001

We returned to the hotel a few hours later, where the party was just beginning. Our room was next door to the hospitality suite and on the same floor as the celebrity guests. Everyone descended on the hospitality suite for more drinking, music and conversation, when Shannon Elizabeth and Joe Reitman (her then-fiancé) arrived. Joe strapped on his inline skates and went from room to room visiting friends. It was hilarious, like summer camp for adults, with poor Aaron as the camp counselor. At one point, I overheard him asking someone on the production crew to try talking to some of the celebrities and settling things down. "All we need is some paying guest complaining to our host hotel that an unruly celebrity here for the *cancer benefit* woke them up by *rollerblading* up and down the halls over his room!"

When all the celebrities retired to their hotel rooms, an impromptu production meeting ensued. Britt and I and the rest of the crew discussed the musical guests (the "talent") and the songs they would perform. They brought up an artist named Uncle Kracker, whose appearance was still contingent on his ability to arrive late in the afternoon the next day, rehearse, perform and fly back out again immediately after the show. As they talked about the songs he would perform, his hit "Follow Me" was the obvious choice.

Then Antonio suggested Uncle Kracker perform "Drift Away," by Mentor Williams (made famous by Dobie Gray), a song he'd heard him perform at a recent show. He had a fax of the song in his hand from the artist's management, which he offered to sing, to jog everyone's memory. "Feel free to sing with me, if you know it," he said amid snickers from his crew pals. "I can use all the help I can get." He couldn't sing very well, but I knew immediately what song he was singing, so being the singer of all tunes that I am (it's true), I began to sing along.

Oh, give me the beat, boys, and free my soul
I want to get lost in your rock and roll
And drift away.

After more chuckles and sarcastic comments, the decision was made. It was unanimous. If Uncle Kracker made it into town for the show, he would do both numbers. I like to think I actually helped, because truly, Antonio couldn't carry a tune. But if all I did was score some points with him, it was all good.

The next day we looked forward to the evening's Mint Jubilee show and gala benefit. Our schedule was fairly tight, with more rehearsals as well as press conferences at the John Brown Cancer Research Center. At about four o'clock we returned to our hotel to prep for the evening, a black-tie affair. Britt's wardrobe had arrived, and it was exquisite.

I knew I hadn't looked so good in years, but I also knew I would have to work some magic just to keep up. I dressed in one of her extra gowns, a black number with sheer strips running through it. It flattered my figure (which was lean, but—uh, er—*loose* in places). The dress held everything in just so and I felt like a million bucks.

The show was excellent. Uncle Kracker arrived to perform both numbers and everyone loved him. Afterward, the rest of the evening turned into the full gala affair it was known for and we partied the night away. I was able to sneak in a few dances with Antonio when Britt and I weren't fluttering about. We shared drinks and interesting conversations with celebrities and her friends throughout the night.

Britt, to my right with several of the gang of new friends just after the Mint Jubilee Gala, 2001

When the guests departed, we (the show crew, celebrity guests, and a few others) went out to Bar Louisville, where a roped-off section was set up for us, the VIPs. It was yet another fantastic gathering as we mingled and laughed with new friends, celebrities, and others, making conversation and enjoying several mint juleps, the official drink of the upcoming Kentucky Derby. There were a few other nightlife stops after Bar Louisville, because, as I discovered, Louisville is the *real* city that never sleeps.

I felt bad for Sheriff Bob and the others, who must have been exhausted. At one point, I offered to buy them hotdogs from one of the street vendors, but they politely declined. Finally, at about two-thirty or three in the morning, we returned to our hotel.

Once we arrived, the entire group of us landed in the hospitality suite and realized a very important thing: we were famished! The suite's stock of M&Ms and peanuts just wouldn't do. We'd all nibbled at the dinner that evening, but in all the excitement had forgotten to really eat something worthwhile during the festivities.

Someone made a quick run to White Castle for the slimiest, greasiest excuse for burgers I have ever swallowed. Britt told me they were called *sliders*, because they go down your throat like oil (yup, that's where the term comes from). I hesitated for a second, because I'd been so strict on my diet, but *she* was rail-thin and eating them up, and well, I was hungry. I decided I had burned plenty of calories on adrenaline alone, so those things went down my throat faster than motor oil!

After an incredible evening, I actually went back to my room that night a little disappointed. I know. Unbelievable. Antonio and I had a chance to actually talk a little. I learned he lived in Los Angeles, was divorced with a son the same age as my younger son and that he and his ex-wife had a very amicable arrangement. He seemed like a very interesting person, and we had this amazing chemistry. He'd clearly shown he was attracted to me, that the feeling was mutual, yet we'd both reluctantly said good night outside of the elevator after we all left the hospitality suite. Here I was, just five months separated from my husband, and I was hot for this guy. But I hadn't felt this way in so *long* and it felt *good*. I wanted desperately to do something about it. I walked into my room with a disappointed look on my face, where Britt was already getting ready for bed.

"Oh! Hey! In a few minutes, Brian is coming over!" she said happily. She was giving me the "heads up." We were in a suite and she would be closing her doors for the evening, once he arrived. Brian was one of the show producers, the one she mentioned earlier and with whom she'd had an on-again-off-again romance over the last couple of years.

"Okay." I said glumly.

When she realized I didn't gush with her about Brian, she asked "What's wrong, sweetie?" After a second I blurted out "I *so* wanted to kiss Antonio! He's SO sexy and we have this incredible chemistry! But we just said good night!"

Britt looked at me like a first-grade schoolteacher who was giving me the "tsk tsk."

"Well, just go over to his room right now!" she said. I wasn't sure if she was serious, or just wanted to get rid of me to have the room to share with Brian.

"Are you kidding? What would I say? I can't go over there!" I insisted.

"Of course you can!" she replied, "Listen. I am a firm believer in going after what you want. Besides, we are here on this incredible weekend to enjoy ourselves and have a blast. It's not like you are hoping to have a meaningful relationship with this guy, is it? No. Of course it isn't. So march over there and tell him you can't sleep, that you are too excited and ask him if he wants to stay up with you for a while."

Well, she definitely knows how to put it, I thought as I closed our door and turned toward his room. She was right, though, damn it! I deserved to do exactly what I wanted this weekend!

I started to march over there like she said. For about two steps. Then my "march" turned into what felt like the slow and painful Exodus from Egypt. My legs could hardly move and felt like lead weights. It was suddenly unbearably hot. (*is the heater on out here in the hallway? It was so much cooler back in my room!*) My heart pounded wildly. My palms were sweating. The hallway became a kaleidoscopic blur. I stopped halfway there—it was only three doors down—to make a sacrifice to a golden calf. I needed a panic room, but it was so *me*. *Dammit! I always jump first and ask questions later!* Eventually I found myself in front of his door, not knowing what to do. *Screw it!* I thought. *Here goes nothin'.*

"Hi." I said when he answered the door, as if he would know why I was there. "I just, well, I…" I stammered. He interrupted me by stepping backward toward the sofa in his room and turning the lights off. I wasn't quite sure what he was doing, but as the light from the open door streamed across his gorgeous Latin face, he motioned for me to come and lie down with him on the couch. I did. I was whispering about how "I just couldn't sleep," and "I was too excited to let it all be over," when he shut me up by kissing me. His lips were full and perfect and *it* was perfect. As I kissed him back, I realized I had not enjoyed kissing *anyone* for many, many years, and oh how I missed it! *This is good. This is really good*, I thought to myself. For someone who was "married for life" just a few months back and wasn't quite yet divorced, this was not only good. This was gigantically, enormously awesome. I was hooked and I wanted. I wanted it all. The lips, the kisses and the attention from this guy, if I could get it.

It was about that time that Antonio's roommate got up from the inside bedroom, opened his door, and noisily went into the bathroom. He was letting us know, as the drawers slammed in the bathroom and the faucet turned on full-blast, that he could hear us and he wasn't happy about it. It was time for me to go, but I didn't care a bit. I kissed Antonio good night as I floated back to my room. I was elated. I was the happiest girl on planet earth, even if I had to go back to my room and interrupt my girlfriend in her little hookup. At least I could sleep with a smile on my face, knowing there was still the Derby to attend and another night left to this dreamy weekend.

And They're Off!

"Um, excuse me ... Do you think Kid ... I mean, Mr. Rock would allow my gorgeous girlfriend to take a picture with him? She wants to prove to her son that she was here."

It seemed as if my head had just hit the pillow, when it was time to wake up again and prepare for the Kentucky Derby. I hadn't slept much anyway, so I popped right out of bed, exuberant and excited over my little (and I mean little) hookup from the night before. I remembered kissing Antonio and thinking it was purely spectacular.

Britt and I had much to accomplish before the motorcade would pick us up. We would arrive in style in limos, escorted into Churchill Downs by sheriffs. We still hadn't purchased our derby hats, which are almost as important as the race itself, and we were getting a bit frantic about it. Looking back now, I realize how absurd it was to think we could find the perfect hat on the day of the Kentucky Derby, but off we went with Sheriff Bob to every hat shop, mall and second-hand boutique Louisville had to offer.

We were shopping so long we realized we might actually miss the most important race of the day, so Britt and I finally each settled on a hat and raced back to the hotel to get ready. We'd already missed the motorcade but decided it was better to be fashionably late and look fabulous than to drive with the motorcade looking out of place.

As "talent," we drove right up to a walkway leading to our box seats in the stands at Churchill Downs. The sheriffs' cars had full access to the grounds and could go where no other cars could. We found we weren't late at all. Many others in our group were just arriving as well, which was a relief to both of us.

The box seats at Churchill Downs had menu service, waiters and a full bar. We watched the race with all the other celebrities, even those who hadn't come to the Mint Jubilee, like Pamela Anderson, Kid Rock, Courteney Cox and David Arquette. Kid Rock had a full security staff with him, but Britt arranged for me to take a picture with him to show my older son, who was a music buff and would know who he was. Coming out of the shelter of my little wifey-dom, I had no clue. I knew Joel would never believe I was that close to Kid Rock without the picture. Once we got the go-ahead—which apparently was a big deal, because Kid Rock doesn't like to be bothered by fans—I started to make my way over. As I edged into the group, I turned slightly and came within inches of Pamela Anderson's face. She was shorter than me (which is short, really), and I must say, she had the most incredible beauty I'd ever seen, especially close up. She wasn't wearing her usual stage or television makeup, and she looked fresh, sun-kissed and in love. I will never forget that. All my preconceived notions of this woman were blown to hell. She looked so natural and pretty. I quickly turned, stooped down to Kid and thanked him, smiled for Britt as she snapped the photo, and it was done.

Me and the Kid (I know, he's thrilled!)

Britt and I located our little group and sat at a table with Antonio and another couple. We drank mint juleps until it was time to place our bets for the big race. I think I won twelve dollars when *Monarchos* won the race, but I'd borrowed the cash from Antonio and split the proceeds with him, so my big winnings were really a whopping six bucks. The whole betting thing—not to mention horse racing—was a first for me but hey, I was a *winner*! I was thrilled.

We followed the group to the paddock for group photos with some of the most successful names in television, along with the winning horse. It was like a dream.

The end of our day at the Kentucky Derby was actually a little sad, as we were approaching the end of this incredible weekend. I got the sense that this was not a normal weekend for the crew and celebrities either, nor would any of us soon forget it.

Britt and I had such a great time, we missed our sheriff and the motorcade (again, dammit!). We'd been so distracted by the festivities and fun that we hadn't noticed the time. We hitched a ride with Antonio and his roommate's sheriff back to the hotel, by then feeling more than a little tipsy.

I have learned that every fantastic party, weekend affair, or gala does not go without its share of drama. As we rode back in the crammed mini-SUV, I sat in the back seat, and Britt, who was very affected by the combination of alcohol and heat, climbed into the back with Antonio. I watched as my tipsy girlfriend grew more and more affectionate toward the guy I was into. It was nothing spectacular—just a few caresses on his arm, but I could tell he was pretty tipsy as well. He was liking the attention, and I didn't like what I was seeing. My sober mind would have known that Britt meant absolutely nothing by it. I knew she was affectionate with everyone, and even more so when she drank, but at the time, this was not okay with me. I felt wounded and upset.

When we arrived at the hotel, I left the car without a word and rushed to our room. We'd all agreed it would be a good idea to try and nap for a few hours before getting ready again and heading to the post-Derby party. I was silent as I walked back, and Britt caught up, trying to chat casually. I couldn't imagine ever doing such a thing to a girlfriend and I was livid that she had allowed herself to get out of control like that. I was in no mood for a casual chat or to make nicey-nice.

She knew I was upset and tried to prod me into discussing it. I too was affected by the drinks and acted dramatic and extreme. "Don't even talk to me," I said coldly. "No matter what you say, it'll never be good enough! You have your hands full of men and you decide to climb all over the guy I am interested in right in the back of the SUV! And right in front of me!" She cried and expressed her sorrow, but I would have nothing of it. Of course, she hadn't climbed all over Antonio, but I was not about to let her know that. Not until after my nap.

At about six that evening, I heard some rustling in the room and realized Britt had woken and was rummaging through her things to get ready. I rolled over with a moan. I just wanted to sleep forever and never deal with any drama. She came over to the side of the bed.

"Lisa," she pleaded, "I am so sorry! I don't know what got into me. You have every right to be upset with me. I was very affected by the drinks. I'm still affected. I don't know what else to say." She began to cry again.

My back was to her, and my eyes were open now. I breathed in and let out a heavy sigh as I rolled over. "I just don't need people in my life who don't respect me. Whether they are drunk or not, it makes no difference to me." I explained. "So, I guess you have to decide if you want to be in my life and I have to decide if I can trust you in my life."

It was a very uncomfortable conversation, but it needed to happen. Britt was and is a gorgeous woman. I don't worry now about my looks, because with age comes a certain comfort and security if you work for it. But back then I felt very fragile. We cried a lot, but we both agreed emphatically that we wanted to stay friends and move past this. Admittedly, I was not yet over it completely, but I was willing to let bygones be bygones for the rest of the weekend. When I say I will let it go, that is what I do. I let Britt know that she hadn't really climbed all over Antonio, which relieved her. Much to her credit, amid disappointments and tears, she was also able to pull it all together and we got through the evening as friends.

That night, our last full night in Louisville, we were all invited to the home of MJ Diebold, whose husband was of the Diebold family who founded the now famous locks and security company. Look at the emblem on the sliding contraption that comes to you at the bank drive-through, and you will know the Diebolds I am talking about). She was a very nice, enthusiastic socialite who opened up her home on the river to the hundreds who came that night.

Aaron Anderson, who was becoming a favorite of mine for his hilarious, elaborate stories, greeted us at the door to tell us how former *MTV* on-camera host Daisy Fuentes had walked through the house the previous year and said, with a look of awe, "It looks like Versace came in and threw up all over the place."

She had a point: there were leopard prints, brass and black lacquered accents everywhere, but I wouldn't say Versace *threw up* there. Maybe he broke a sweat all over the place.

The party was catered, with open bars in some of the extra bathrooms. MJ's master bedroom had a karaoke system set-up. It was actually pretty bizarre to hang out in this woman's room, which featured an elevated, giant round bed covered in leopard-print duvet and linens. There were ornate statues and black lacquered accessories aplenty, as well as a disco ball hanging from center ceiling. At first I wondered if everyone was creeped out by it, but soon enough this unique karaoke room was the hit of the party. It was where everyone ended up to dance, try to sing Janis Joplin or Whitney Houston tunes, and laugh a lot. Antonio and I reconnected and I never mentioned a word about his little exchange with Britt. I knew I wanted nothing serious from him, so I was not going to press a single thing. I had no claims on him, nor did I want them. I did want *him*, though. We kissed a little between dances and my fluttering around the party with Britt.

Once the focus moved to MJ's bedroom, the fun took a new turn. We watched French Stewart and Katherine La Nasa sing a fun duet. Chloe Sevigny got up with her beau, and many others performed as well. Then all the girls and guys got together and sang "Summer Lovin'" Grease-style. After that little episode, we took a break and the dance music came back on. We danced into the night until about four in the morning, before heading back to the hotel for some much-needed sleep.

Sunday was our true day of rest, when we (the remaining crew, along with Britt and I) went to the Louisville Slugger museum. I bought an authentic bat for Graden, whom I missed horribly. I was eager to return and cuddle up with him.

On Monday morning, we flew home. Britt and I talked some more and she told me just how important our friendship was to her. It was some good girl time. We laughed about some of the funny stories of the weekend until we landed at LAX.

Back in Orange County, I put together a photo album of my weekend in Louisville to preserve the incredible memories as well as the anticipation of what may yet come around the next corner of my life. In just a couple of days, I was exposed to a whole new world of people who loved life and lived it to the fullest. I met men and women who paid attention to me, gave credence to my ideas, and accepted me for who I was, even though I was sure they initially thought I was a mousy, timid thing. These were all creative, intelligent, youthful, successful people. Most were very attractive and it was not just a physical attraction, but an attraction to their personalities and charisma, which made them magnetic and hard to resist. Antonio and I had exchanged phone numbers and promised to be in touch, and I was now determined to make it happen.

The trip to Louisville changed me forever. My "fantastic" corporate job was suddenly mind-numbing and monotonous. Everything had lost its shimmer. I realized that, though I'd always believed we must do what we love or we're bound to fail, I'd also acted on the compulsion to find security fast. I'd let the dream die once Marcus and I separated. I'd done the best I could with the opportunities given me in an emergency situation, and I knew the corporate job was the right thing to do. But I also knew that these sneak peeks into opportunities and possibilities happened for a reason. My eyes had been opened! I wanted something different, and I wanted to find a way to achieve it soon. I was not content to stay in my corporate world and I was pumped with adrenaline, realizing that though I was only thirty-five years old and it *wasn't* too late to move into a new career, I was *thirty-five*, and time was ticking. Even though I had always wanted to work in television or film, I had never been able to really pursue it. I knew if I wanted it at this stage of my life, it was time to move on it.

On top of that, life in South Orange County seemed quite provincial and "white bread" to me (not that there is anything wrong with that). I just longed for the cultural diversity of a large city, the creative thoughts and people that a city could attract and all a large city had to offer.

After a month or two of ho-humming about, I decided to do whatever it would take to move to Los Angeles and work in the television industry. I'd put my hopes and dreams aside for too long, and now it was *my* turn. No matter how young everyone else in "the business" seemed, I was feeling younger and more empowered by the day, and I felt the timing was perfect.

I put together a plan:

1. Communicate: Tell my showbiz girlfriend Britt, and anyone else who was remotely connected to the industry, of my plan and elicit any possible advice or assistance.

2. Network, network, network: Express interest in attending whatever events and/or parties possible with same friends/acquaintances. Go to ALL such events, collect names, phone numbers and information. Organize and plan to take care of childcare and other concerns.

3. Visualize my reality: Whenever possible, on weekends or other holidays, go up to Los Angeles with my son and do something fun: drive to the beach, rent bikes, watch a movie, take walks on the boardwalk, whatever. Start to imagine what our *whole* life in Los Angeles will look like (friends, activities, opportunities). Picture those things and don't let go of those images.

4. Stalk (I mean, stay in contact with) my new friends: Get in touch with Aaron and see where that leads. Visit Antonio as much as possible (*duh…HOTTIE*) and continue to meet other industry people from the connection with him as well.

My life was moving forward once again. I knew I would soon make the move to the City of the Angels, and that prospect alone was exhilarating. Each time I acted on my plan, I felt like I was one step closer.

Fit To Be Tied...Up

"You just kept sitting on Ron Harper's lap, with his bodyguard saying 'Lisa! Lisa!' and him saying, 'No. It's okay!' It was so hilarious!"—Britt

"Lis ..." my beyond-tipsy girlfriend tried to chide me, "Don't call him again. He invited us to *Joya* to meet him, but he wasn't there. Just let it go. You don't want to come on too strong."

What on earth is she talking about, "Come on too strong?" I was a woman in need of some immediate affection, and by god, I was going to have it!

I'd just spent the last seven hours getting gorgeous and trekking through Beverly Hills in four-inch strappy stilettos to get to one of the trendiest nightspots at the time, all to meet Antonio, for godsakes. Get real! Did she really think I'd give up now?

Come on too strong! Pffff!

Antonio had shown me that I was sexy and attractive again. It was of no consequence that he happened to be incredibly hot. Okay, it was. But I wanted *really badly* to get lucky and he was the one I wanted. Besides, Antonio was a grown man, with an ex-wife and a son of his own. He was old enough to know what he was doing and he certainly knew when a woman was interested. Regular women send signals. Me? I conk men upside the head with a proposition impossible to misunderstand or ignore, let alone refuse. Yep. I had always employed the good ole' cave-girl tactic. I saw no need to divert from that course now.

Our time at *Joya* was quite an adventure and lots of fun, aside from just missing Antonio there. The owner was one of Antonio's friends and had put us on "the list" to get in.

This "list" thing is a whole other interesting factor in Los Angeles. I have found that in the city, there are actually two types of "lists." There is the list that actually means something, where friends of the owner, people with connections or other important people are allowed to jump the line and enter the club immediately upon arrival. If you are on this list, you are considered somewhat of a VIP and are treated as one. Then there is the list I like to call the Pretty People list. This list is found mostly in the largest cities like Los Angeles and New York. Don't get me wrong: if you are on this list, congratulations! It means you are considered hot enough by event producers and club promoters to stand out in front of their club and make them look good.

Nightclubs like to have a line outside, but *who* stands in that line is as important as the line itself. So, if a club promoter or event person places you on a list, be prepared to wait in line along with the rest of the other "listees." The good news is you will probably get in at some point, giving you an opportunity to see and be seen by some of the most famous people in town who happen to be walking past you into the VIP section of the club. If you go to a trendy nightclub in Los Angeles or New York and you aren't on any kind of list, then you'd better plan on joining the other less fortunate lining up in the back alley behind the bar, sharing all manner of concoctions and smoking cigarettes. It's not half bad, if you like to meet interesting people and don't mind the smoke. There are definitely some fascinating characters standing in line at the *true* back of the bar.

When we arrived at *Joya*, it turned out that my girlfriend knew the owner as well. We were given the five-star treatment, with full access to the back room for VIPs. It was fun to jump the line and be escorted right in, but I felt a tinge of sadness for the others I left behind… just a tinge.

It was a fun night out with the girls and the VIP room had its share of industry people and celebrities. We met and got friendly with NBA star (at the time) Ron Harper. I didn't notice then, but my friends later told me that Harper's bodyguard kept asking me to back away from him, but he was more than gracious and allowed the delusional flirtation to continue. At one point, I was sitting on the basketball player's lap, much to his bodyguard's chagrin. He kept saying things like, "Lisa, don't do that. Lisa, you need to get up." To which Ron would say, "It's okay, it's okay."

I told Britt later that Ron was the one who put me on *his* lap to save me from tripping over his monstrous feet. Yeah. I could put up a smokescreen even while tipsy.

"I never would have let it go anywhere," I insisted to my girlfriend later. It was all in fun, and a-okay since it was girls' night—no one treads on girls' night.

At about two in the morning, Antonio and I finally spoke again. He had moved on to a house party in Hollywood. Though he invited us to join him, we were already at my girlfriend's house and were not going out again. I'm sure my friend wondered whether I'd lost all sense of self-control and would hop in a cab to chase this guy down, but I do have my limits. It was disappointing to me, but I was encouraged by the promise of getting together with Antonio the next evening. He asked me to come by his place and have some dinner. Graden was at a sleepover with a friend back in our little Orange County neighborhood and could spend the next night at home with his nanny.

Though I could have made arrangements with Graden's friend or the nanny so I could stay up in Los Angeles once morning came, I made the trek back home bright and early to hang out with Graden all day. In my mind, my little indulgence was all on me. I could suck up the extra round-trip drive the next night, if getting lucky was all that important. Besides, I would miss my little dude. Not going home wasn't even a consideration.

I'll cut to the chase: the next night, I drove back up to LA, to Antonio's place, knowing full well what I wanted. I wanted that same feeling I got when I'd kissed him in Louisville—the kind where the hair on the back of your neck rises and you get goose bumps and warm tingly feelings all over. I craved something that may or may not result in sex, but I wanted it soon! I'd had a taste of passion in Louisville and I wanted more. I was on my way to a divorce and was happy to be single. I had no desire to jump into a relationship—the idea actually nauseated me—nor did I think I had any business doing so. My therapist encouraged me to have some fun and allow myself these little pleasures, so I decided I would.

Antonio had prepared a fantastic dinner by the time I got to his place on the beach. I nibbled a little but really couldn't think of food. After dinner, we took our Makers (my favorite bourbon) with us, walked out onto the upstairs balcony and kissed. It was unbelievably passionate again and I was enjoying every minute, when he suddenly broke away for a second to tell me about his life.

Really? His life? Now?

I didn't understand how he could so easily put the brakes on the passion and kill the buzz by bringing up a topic like that. Just when things were going so perfectly, somehow he thinks that *now* is the time to tell me about his life! When women do it, guys complain and say things like, "Can you believe it? She wanted to talk!" But, in my opinion, it's worse when a man does it. Why? Because men are *constantly* complaining about how women have the upper hand in the battle of the sexes, how "in-control" women are of how much sex goes on in a relationship. There's no argument here. I agree. So, when I'm hot and heavy, why would a guy want to bring it to a screeching halt and start a conversation?

Even in this moment of passion, I was able to see the forest for the trees. I knew it was Antonio's small, last-minute attempt to absolve himself of responsibility for this little exchange. He figured if he let me in on his secrets or something, the ball was then in my court. *Okay,* I thought, *bring it.* Because tonight I didn't really care what he said. Oh, I listened as he told me he'd just broken up with his girlfriend, whom he'd been with for a few years, blah, blah, blah, I nodded as he explained they'd been apart for a while, yadda, yadda, yadda. It was when he said he did *not* want to get into another relationship that I smiled broadly.

"That's perfect!" I said. "My sentiments exactly!" He looked at me and searched my eyes wondering if I was for real. They smiled back, full of playfulness and glee.

"Really?" he asked.

"Really. I swear! Cross my heart," I said, as I crossed my heart. "I am not even divorced yet. I have no business in a relationship, so this is just fine by me."

"Oh, I get it." he surmised, mischievously. "You just want me to fuck you, don't you?"

I looked at him, and as my lips curled up into a sly smile, I quipped, "Yep. Among other things," He kissed me again, took my hand and we started downstairs.

We had only taken a few steps when (and doesn't this just top it all), my heart started palpitating. My palms got pasty. I was a suddenly a nervous wreck. *What IS it with this guy and the palpitations? What is it with me not thinking these things through!* What on earth was I going to do? I was still *incredibly* self-conscious about my body. I was nervous about this gorgeous man, who'd obviously been around the block, seeing me naked.

There was still so much work to be done! The weight loss had done its job, but so had gravity. My boobs were now more like shriveled pomegranates, and my belly, well, it was flat all right, thanks to the intense ab regimen I'd put myself through most of my adult life. But there was this other issue. I'd had a vertical c-section (yes, *vertical*) in the delivery of Graden, and the aftermath was not pretty. There were these things I called my "curtains": loose skin, hanging down from this six-inch vertical scar. The scar was a well-earned memento of the beauty of motherhood that nature (and the doctors) had bestowed on me.

These deformities looked more like something you would see in a Wes Craven horror movie than on a would-be sex kitten. Can you imagine? I could just see it: me, dressed up in sexy lingerie, maybe even some out-of-control high-heels, with a g-string and garters. Then, just as I'm about to undress completely, saying in the most smoldering tone possible, "Hey, there, big boy! What do you think of these bodacious ta-tas?" flashing my shriveled fruit, "and how about these baby scars?" It made me cringe. But as Antonio approached the deep beyond of the downstairs—and possibly even his bedroom—it was all I could do to maintain my composure.

But as we drew nearer the base of the stair, I found my composure and quickly elaborated a "plan B," one that didn't sound contrived or as though I was chickening out. We walked into the downstairs bedroom, and he was all over me.

"For tonight," I began, between kisses, "Let's take it slow."

"Whatever you like."

Wow, that was easy, I thought. Now I *was* in charge. Men are right! I was able to take charge with just one little statement! Ha! Though I was dressed in an incredibly cute little surfer-style mini skirt and tee shirt, the only thing that came off was my tee, *and* I kept my bra on, thank you! I decided at that point that I wanted to see what *he* was made of. I wanted to have a look at his body. He was amazingly accommodating of my every wish.

I undressed him and began a mission of discovery. As my hand moved across his smooth skin, I could feel the definition of every muscle. It was incredibly passionate and erotic. I found myself enjoying pleasing him. It felt good to know I could do that and not lose myself at the same time. It was exciting and thrilling to learn that sex between two consenting adults could be so much more than, well, just sex. Antonio and I *both* were enjoying my explorations of his body and him. He, in turn, was perfectly content to be the little science experiment that opened up a whole new world for me.

As we lay together, our hormones calm once again, there was no hint of awkwardness. It was as if we had come to some great understanding and were both taking in the sheer bliss. How lucky was I? I remember thinking to myself *I don't ever have to wonder whether or not I am desirable. I now know this. I am on a great path of discovery. I'm a frickin' explorer! And, I can continue to grow and learn and experience all that life has to offer!* I was determined from that moment on to live and enjoy every aspect of life and do it completely, to experience new things whenever given the chance. I drove home that night feeling empowered and really great about myself. *This is the start of a wonderful thing* I thought. Maybe I was simply satisfied hormonally but hell, the satisfaction counted for a ton in my book.

As I shuffled up the stairs at home, my comfy bed beckoned me, but I knew a shower was in order. The warm water felt good on my body. As I looked down at myself, I decided that if I could swing it financially, my body could use a little reconstruction. As much as I loved motherhood with all my heart, birthing children had taken a serious physical toll. I made a mental note to start thinking about what and where to have things done as I crawled into bed. My head sank into my comfortable pillow and I drifted off. This thing with Antonio was fabulous, to be sure, but more importantly, so was my new outlook on life. It felt absolutely spectacular.

Project Runway Could Be My Bitch

"That guy is a lucky man. If things don't work out with you guys, I'll be the first to get in line!"—Mini Brad Pitt

One of my favorite TV shows is *Project Runway*. I love the way creative and talented designers create beautiful, hip and trendy looks with a specific event or person in mind. They must put the *entire* look and feel together, from the shoes and accessories, to the outfit, the hair and the makeup, keeping the week's unique challenge in mind. Whether it is a look for the jet set, a simple summer cocktail dress or an evening gown all constructed from recycled corrugated plastic, it must come together with purpose, and be practical and pleasing to the eye.

I'm sure the reason I like the show is because I can relate to it (I must say: this is my *forte*). Women have faced these kinds of "designing" challenges for eons. I am known among my friends for having a knack for creating something spectacular (or hey, at least *credible*) from virtually nothing. Once I have the overall "look and feel" of the challenge (or event) in mind, I can usually pull it off.

Antonio and I had been seeing each other for about a month or so, enjoying whatever slices of adventurous time we could steal together, when he called one day with a plan for a little rendezvous. He wanted to meet me in Long Beach to stay the night.

Really? Long Beach?

The only things I remembered about Long Beach were its oil rigs and dingy downtown streets, but the last time I'd been there I think I was twelve, visiting my sister and her husband, so what did I know?

The plan was for me to drive up from Orange County and he would drive down from Los Angeles. Antonio knew the popular little strip of bars and restaurants well. He made reservations at a cute little hotel within walking distance of the strip, and our date was set.

That was all I needed to immediately set my creation, or Project *Rendezvous*, into motion. I was going to make this an incredibly romantic and sensual evening. I was still working at my corporate job at the time, so I had to pull some strings to leave work early enough to set everything up.

On the day of the challenge, um, rendezvous, I left work at two o'clock and ran into the gourmet market nearby. Antonio and I were meeting at a trendy little crab shack near the hotel at six, so I had to move fast. I envisioned a room with candlelight, sumptuous fresh fruit, cheese and crackers, gourmet chocolates, some sensual oils and the perfect background music. I ran home to change clothes.

My outfit was of the utmost importance. It would set the tone for the entire evening. I thought about the outfit for days and shopped around Laguna Beach and Mission Viejo for just the right accents, finally putting together the perfect ensemble. I wanted Antonio to be awestruck, or at least greatly aroused (preferably both) when he saw me.

I slipped into the sizzling black corset I'd purchased, some sexy underwear, black stockings and garters. Then I put the sexy business skirt and jacket I'd worn to work back on over the lingerie. *I wonder if I should wear a blouse over the corset*, I thought. *Nah!* My jacket covered the corset completely and added a little mystery to the presentation. Finally, I slipped on the sexiest stilettos I owned. *Wow!* I thought as I looked in the mirror. *It's amazing how great a suit can look by adding a few sexy accents!*

I thought about the first time Antonio and I had really been "together," at his place in Los Angeles and how I was so self-conscious about my body. My self-consciousness was still there and so were my shriveled pomegranates, but we'd been able to get past that obstacle, thankfully!

Actually, it was pretty funny the first time I let him see me naked. I had to let him in on my little secret: that my body had been a little used and abused by my infant children. I had nursing-mom boobs and my tummy bore the record of the wonderful work of my obstetrician. Antonio was very nice about it, assuring me that he'd seen nursing-mom boobs before (*whew*) and that my tummy couldn't be *that* bad (*Gee, thanks*). It wasn't a great pep talk, but it worked.

I am more and more amazed at how quickly men can overlook women's physical anomalies more easily than we women ever can, especially when sex is at stake. I find that the more confident and nonchalant we are about our bodies, the more attractive we ladies are to men. Men actually *can* do without the physical perfection and skin-and-bones look of Hollywood starlets as long as their woman is healthy, fit and comfortable in her own skin.

At the time of my Project Rendezvous, I had been sticking to my diet and was losing weight steadily each week. I was actually getting thin again! It was particularly gratifying to finally be able to fit back into smaller clothing, so I felt especially confident that day. *What a difference from six months ago!*

"Never again," I said out loud, looking directly into my eyes in the mirror, like a mother admonishing her child.

I was thrilled about how things were going. It made all the work easier, like a snowball effect: I lost some weight, liked it, worked harder, lost more weight, loved the way I looked in a new pair of jeans, lost more weight, and things just kept going! At one point I almost thought I would keep losing weight no matter what I did, just from the sheer adrenaline rush of my new life. Of course I knew it wasn't true, but getting and staying in shape became easier every day, the more I continued to stick to it.

Dressed and feeling sexy, I ran downstairs, grabbed the romantic music CDs I'd set aside in the morning along with my portable CD player and speakers and loaded them into my car. Yep. Speakers. A CD player. That's what it took back in the day (just a few years ago, really) to create ambiance in your hotel room. We had no iPod docks, music-listening stations, or smart phones back then, no.

I chatted for a bit with the nanny to make sure everything was set for Graden's buddy to sleep over that night. I gave her money to order pizza, kissed and hugged Graden and was out the door. I knew I would not be gone all night, even though we had a room. It was more about the rendezvous than an overnight vacation in Long Beach, anyway. Antonio and I both knew it and that was all part of the fun and excitement. I planned to be home later, sleep in my own bed, and wake up on a Saturday morning to spend a nice leisurely day with my son and his friend.

I drove up to the hotel, and the valet came to park my car while a bellboy inquired about my luggage. He came up to the window, and it felt as though he looked right down into the opening of my jacket. *Does he know what I'm up to?* I wondered as I slid out of my car, careful not to reveal the garters underneath my skirt.

He was boyish, sweet and flirtatious. And he had a cute sort of young Brad Pitt look to him. I handed him the bags from the gourmet market, my CDs, candles, CD player and speakers and walked toward the front desk. I giggled inwardly knowing these items just *had* to be screaming "torrid love-fest" to him, but he tried to make casual conversation and asked what I was in town for. *Yeah, as if you don't know.* I told him I was meeting my boyfriend. So, I lied. Sometimes it's just easier to say what you think they want to hear. Okay, maybe *he* would've wanted to hear the down and dirty truth.

We walked to the front desk, and I let the clerk know that I wanted to go and set the room up, if I could. He allowed it when I showed him my credit card, and little Brad Pitt and I were off to the elevator.

"So, what are you meeting your boyfriend for?" he began, then quickly realized it was a little intrusive and added, "If you don't mind my asking, that is?"

I smiled reassuringly. "Just a little getaway." Then I decided to give just a bit more without giving it all away. "We aren't really a couple, yet," I added. "It's all pretty new."

"Well, he's a lucky guy," mini-Brad replied, smiling from ear to ear. *So cute and sweet.* I looked at his name tag. *Dillon* was from Michigan. Of course his name was Dillon! It was perfect! I was quite sure that if he ever got out of Long Beach and into Hollywood, I would see him on some CW show in the near future.

The bell for the floor rang, and Dillon led me to my room. I walked around while he showed me the standard amenities. The clock read 5:30 PM. I started taking things out of the bags. I was in a time crunch now—only fifteen minutes to set up and another fifteen to freshen up and get to the restaurant. Yikes!

"So, what do you think?" the bellboy said, jolting me from my thoughts.

"What? Oh! Everything looks great!" I hurriedly replied.

"Awesome!" Dillon said with a smile as he started toward the door. "Like I said, that guy is a lucky man. If things don't work out with you guys, I'd be the first to get in line."

"Well, thank you." I managed to say as I tipped him, and he gave a half-wave and awkwardly, but oh-so-adorably walked out the door.

I plopped onto the bed. I had left my house feeling confident that I looked good, but this was a surprise. Was confidence the answer to attracting good-looking men? I felt no conceit, only shock and surprise. Dillon's little proposition was not just out-of-left field. It was out of nowhere! *Wow*, I said to myself. That was it. Nothing else. Just wow. And then I smiled, happy to know I still had "it" at the ripe old age of thirty-six.

I quickly set up the music center beside a luscious platter of strawberries, blackberries, cherries, chocolates, crackers and cheese. I set out the candles and placed the sensual oils to be ready for use. I put my favorite disc on auto-repeat, freshened up in front of the mirror and stepped out the door to meet Antonio.

It was a beautiful night with clear skies. The air was crisp and cool. The ocean breeze was soothing and silky. I smiled. *What a great night for a rendezvous!*

When Antonio walked into the restaurant, I stood up from the bar stool I'd been perched on. He greeted me with a smile, grabbed both hands, and as he leaned in to give me a kiss, said, "Wow! You look amazing!"

"Thank you." I replied. I couldn't wait for him to see the room. What a wonderful evening this was turning into!

As we walked together toward the hotel, my anticipation grew. I was so excited to see the look on Antonio's face when he entered the room. When we got to the hotel lobby, I casually mentioned to him that I'd already checked us in. I had a coy little grin on my face.

"You did, eh? What have you been up to?" he asked, looking at me, scanning for a clue.

"You'll see." I smiled.

All of my scheming and efforts paid off. I asked Antonio to wait in the hall while I gave the room the candlelit glow I was after and adjusted the music volume. Then I led him in.

I have to add here that I agree with the sentiments of people who plan their weddings. Don't get me wrong, this was nothing *close* to a wedding. In formal weddings, a lot of effort goes into choosing the perfect gown, the pomp and circumstance, the flowers, the attendants and the celebration. These are all part of the buildup to the wedding night, when the bride and groom will consummate their union. Sounds like fantasyland these days, I know. But that fantasyland is all over in a matter of seconds when the bride and groom tear off each other's clothes to do the consummating.

Okay, so Antonio and I were no bride and groom. We weren't even boyfriend and girlfriend. We were just two consenting adults having loads of fun together, but in its own way it was magical. It was the stuff fantasies are made of. And it was real-world stuff too. We tore each other's clothes off. My ensemble came off especially fast.

Project Rendezvous was complete. I definitely felt as though I won the challenge.

The "M" In Milf Stands For "Mother"

"Mommy, when are you coming back? I really miss you mommy. Call me back, okay? (Pause) Oh... and mommy?... I love you." —Graden

After listening to this incredibly adorable voicemail—which, of course, gave me that died-and-gone-to-heaven feeling—I felt a pang of sadness. I had no doubt my five-year-old son was curled up in bed when he called. I missed my little guy! I don't recall exactly where I was when I received the message. Probably having a drink with a promising entertainment industry connection. But it caused me to snap back to reality and decide instantly that it was time to take a break from conquering the entertainment world or overnight trysts with Antonio and spend some real time with my boys. Lots of time. Besides, I'd had my fun and then some, my dizzying, life-changing trip to Kentucky and a few well planned getaway dates with Antonio being the most notable. Now it was time for the real world.

I still had plans to move to Los Angeles, but I learned to keep them quiet until more of the pieces of the puzzle were in place. At work where mundane was king, the fax machine was not working properly, the printer was out of ink, and marketing deadlines always loomed, I struggled to stay motivated. I couldn't talk to anyone about the stirring I was feeling inside as I quietly made plans to move, pursue a whole new career in the entertainment industry and create a wonderful life for my new little family.

That voicemail from Graden was just one among many much-needed, acute reminders of my little son's need for his mommy. His daddy had left us for good. From his point of view, his brother was gone, having moved in with his friend's parents, and now his mommy was disappearing as well. Every good mom should know that even the best nannies and friends are no substitute for her child's first true love: Mommy.

I didn't *intend* to rely too heavily on the nanny. But in this moment, I became aware of a distinct imbalance. The marriage to Marcus had taxed me inside and out. My everything—energy, time and heart—had gone into the relationship, while my goals, dreams and desires moved to a back burner so far away, they were on someone else's stove. Once we were separated, I'd viewed this as my big chance… as MY time. To seize the opportunities as they came, I instinctively went back to what I'd known to do years before as a single mom to Joel. *Get a sitter, and get'er done.*

When Joel was a little tyke, I was an up-and-coming entrepreneur in advertising and media. I drove around in my hot little red Nissan 280 zx t-top. Okay, it was a long time ago. I was thin, fit and always dressed in the most stylish clothes. You may laugh at it, but…THIS was crucial to me as I tried to establish a name for myself in a business that was all about image and appearance—marketing and public relations. My best friends were owners of clothing stores, hair salons, you name it, and they were all at the top of their fields in our small town of Albuquerque, New Mexico. They also made sure I always looked and performed at my best. I loved my life back then because it was a life without limits. I knew I could take my career wherever I wanted it to go and the potential was endless.

I remember the most I'd ever spent on clothes at that time was something like three hundred bucks on a cocktail dress from the city's top couture shop to attend the annual Christmas party of my girlfriend, Adrienne Maloof—yes, *the* Adrienne Maloof, of the popular Housewives series, and one of the Sacramento Kings and Palms Casino Maloofs. But back then she was just a girl who was well known in Albuquerque.

Adrienne was the friend I chose to be the maid of honor at my wedding. Our friendship was one of many relationships that had developed as a result of networking for my marketing and public relations business.

I also shopped around town that year for Christmas gifts for my girlfriends: the Nagel painting for one (wow, can you say throwback? That was so long ago!), the beautiful jewelry for another and the perfume for yet another. I was, and still am very proud of my girlfriends. We knew we were all headed for greatness and there would be no stopping us.

When I met Marcus, Joel was just three years old and the light of my life. I was single-parenting, but we were getting along okay. My whirlwind relationship with Marcus took us very quickly to the altar. His ideas of family seemed, on the surface, to match what I'd grown up with, though he came from a small family (he had three siblings) and mine was large (I had ten!) My family members were loud, sarcastic, and loved to laugh. Marcus's family was quiet and sweet, but controlled.

I approached my marriage and family life as I did everything, with good sense and one-hundred-fifty-percent effort. So it was only natural for me, as a dutiful wife, to give up school when the time came to attend to the needs of Marcus (which were immense) and Joel. I willingly closed my business to have the flexibility to travel when Marcus wanted and to help his business succeed. I sacrificed much, but it never seemed to be too great; I did it all so Marcus and I could build a family heritage and what I perceived as beautiful traditions together.

I probably romanticized my own childhood traditions and family heritage and as a result, put unrealistic expectations on how I approached being a mother, but the family I was raised in had been able, despite whatever faults we had, to create some wonderful times together. Memories of fun and fabulous holidays filled my thoughts. And there was never a dull moment. When people called my family's house they would ask if there was a party going on, because the background noise was always so loud and cheerful. I loved to answer the phone and get that question. I would proudly answer, "Oh no! That's just my family. It's like this all the time!"

When the leaves began to turn in the fall, all the kids' hearts would fill with anticipation for the day Mom Hoerner would arrive. She was my dad's mom and what every grandmother is supposed to be—yet she never would allow us to call her grandma. She and her husband Vernon would arrive with dozens of giant jars of homemade fudge, divinity, peanut brittle, cakes, cookies, caramels, and pralines. We never stopped to think how much time she actually spent baking all of those delicious treats. We just gobbled them up.

I always felt as though I was Mom Hoerner's favorite granddaughter. She would shop at the church bazaars every year prior to visiting and bring me piles of "new" (at least to me) clothes that I would dress up in and model for the entire family.

Then there was my mom, Nereide Frances Padalino. She had traveled in the forties with the Gilbert and Sullivan operetta company, performing onstage. With her Rita Hayworth beauty, J.J. Schubert of the Shubert Theatre and many others had given her work.

My mother, at the age of 18 & Mom and Dad during the same period

She met my father at the ripe old age of eighteen in Times Square, and even that chance meeting had storybook overtones. I loved sitting at her feet as she told some of the romantic stories of convincing Mr. Schubert to let her work as an actress for him (she succeeded without ever having to submit to the grueling audition process) and of meeting her future husband. I suppose it is no surprise that I was willing to give up my education and business for Marcus, since my mom had done the very same thing for my dad.

My dad was an only child who never knew his own father. He was an easygoing, music-loving, retired (by the time I came along) military man who loved my mom. He was a gorgeous Texan, with black hair and piercing blue eyes, known as "Tex" as a young adult.

My mom and dad were fun-loving, giving, creative individuals who sacrificed much to give us kids a better life. Our family was a strong force to be reckoned with in the neighborhood, the Sherwoods.

As I've said, we weren't anywhere near perfect, and we had some incredibly scandalous stories come from within our walls, but we seemed to grow up happy and we at least all *seemed* grounded as kids. That was the heritage I'd dreamed of for my own family. I never wanted to have a lot of kids, but I wanted to build wonderful memories. I dreamed of baking holiday treats for my children and their children, of passing fun memories and traditions down to them that they could in turn, share with their kids.

My divorce ended that dream, of course, but it opened the door to an entirely new world. On my own, I was more in control of the path I would take and the legacy I would hand down, and I didn't take that responsibility lightly.

> I want to tell the single moms out there something that no one ever tells you or *any* would-be mothers. As a parent or even someone who envisions having kids one day, you may want to come back to this regularly, especially if you have little ones at home. I hope that what I am about to tell you will change the way you approach those exhausting, trying times as a parent.

Here is a promise: You *are* going to miss and feel a very sad sense of loss over every single stage of your child's life as it goes by. Like the death of a loved one, you will grieve over moments that are gone. Watch the clock. Know that it is moving forward and there is no turning back. Your child is growing (whether it's before your eyes or not) and you cannot take moments back.

Now, before you say, "Oh, that? I've heard that before" or you quickly agree with it in premise and say "Amen Sister! So true!" dig deep within you. I'm not just saying that time is fleeting. It takes some depth of character and wisdom to realize what this is really all about and what's involved.

In every single phase, your child displays unique behaviors based on their personality, habits and capabilities in that one moment. Once the moment is gone, so is, in a sense, that child who possessed those adorable (sometimes annoying, sometimes endearing) habits and abilities. An example of this would be the crawling nine-month-old that gives way to a toddling, running, talking, jumping two- or three-year-old. You are meant to be there and enjoy each of those wonderful moments if you can, but it's good for you to know in advance about the loss you will feel when those moments are gone. It will feel like you've lost that two-year-old, five-year-old, etc. forever.

A woman I once knew illustrated the grief mothers can feel by continuing to have babies. Yep. A succession of babies. She was particularly fond of the baby stage in her kids' lives. Instead of learning to cherish them at every stage, and finding joy or moving on *with* her children and loving them completely as they aged, (which I'm sure she tried to do in her own way), she would simply find a way—even against her husband's wishes—to get pregnant and have more babies. She just couldn't fathom being a mother without a baby! And she was not very attentive to the kids she already had. As a result, her home was always in disarray, with kids running around trying to find or wash their own clothes, putting themselves to bed and so on. After five kids, her husband finally had a vasectomy. The marriage ended when she became pregnant again by someone else.

Now THAT is extreme! But this feeling of loss is a very real emotion every mother grapples with – some better than others!

I can vividly recall Graden when he was a ten-month-old crawling machine, bobbing his head and humming happily as he motored around our home. He was a happy baby, who was quite happy never to walk. He was the baby in the family, so he was held an awful lot and carried around everywhere, and that was how he liked it. When he finally decided to get his walking legs, and grew into his toddler years, I didn't even realize as I tried to encourage him to start walking (as any good parent would) and stopped carrying him around so much, what was happening before my eyes. Graden the baby was going away. He was putting on his daddy's climbing harness and attempting to climb the neighborhood "boulders" and learning to ride his tricycle. And today, that crawling, bobble-headed humming baby boy is gone forever. I miss him so! If I had another day with him, how I would gather up that little bobble head and shower him with kisses, hold him as much as he wanted, cuddle him, never wanting to put him down! I would tickle him and nuzzle him and laugh with tears of joy while he squealed with glee.

I still feel a tinge of loss every time I see another toddler laughing and giggling uncontrollably with his daddy, or struggling to climb a piece of furniture, or crying because he or she doesn't understand what is happening. The feelings of loss are mixed with quiet satisfaction because I shared these moments with my sons, but I still have to hold back the urge to run over and try to offer my own wisdom or make up for lost time with that stranger's child. I miss that little toddling chunk. He was *my* little toddling chunk and I loved squeezing his little thighs and making him happy by merely hugging and cuddling him.

Then, Graden became a little pre-kindergarten and elementary school person. This is a very difficult time for me to think about, because Marcus' struggles with drugs resurfaced when Graden turned three. From this period forward, our family was unraveling and falling apart.

But I scratched, clawed, scrambled, wept and bled my way through that period the best way that I could, given the tools my own parents, self-help books, our church and friends and family had given me. I know my boys are lovely human beings despite it all and that is all I need to know. Do I wish my children had lived the dream, with two happy parents and a life filled with dreams coming true? Of course.

However, I must, balance all of that, as must all parents, with the joys of my present-day kids and relationships I have with them now. Though I miss the unbearably cute four-year-old versions of Graden and Joel, their seven-year-old versions that cracked silly jokes, and the awkward ten-year-olds that wanted desperately to be so cool (don't they all?), I've got to be present and enjoy the moments of today.

It's because of these types of memories that I have chosen to live by my life's motto: "Enjoy every moment."

I am fortunate that I recognized the need to make some changes when I received that adorable voicemail. I was able to take a moment and simply cherish my boys for a short window of time. At times, my older son Joel would reach out by asking to meet for lunch (translation: I'm hungry. Wanna' take me to lunch?). I'd scurry over to his friend's parents' house, or we'd meet somewhere and he'd jump in the car with his latest favorite CD, or talk about a poet or artist he was into. I opened my mind and listened and appreciated his tastes. I feel proud of those times. He is the first person I call now when I need advice or information on music, poetry and so much more. I respect his knowledge of the arts and his passion. I love that and so much more about him.

During that time, Graden and I did special things too. We booked a hotel room at Disneyland (though it was nearby) and had breakfast with Mickey and Pluto, and closed the park down. We stopped by our neighborhood park at least once a week to slide down the enormous slides (those suckers were SCARY. They spanned the entire side of a high, super steep... did I say *steep*... hill), or climb around the Jungle Gym. Yes I would even squeeze my tush into the tubes and knock my knees on the hard plastic platforms to crawl and chase Graden, or allow him to chase and catch me.

For now, my eyes were focused solely on Joel (from a loving, somewhat sad distance) and Graden. There were very few, if any late-night trysts to plan, few, if any industry events to attend, no concern over new connections to make. My sole purpose was piecing back together the shattered glass of our lives. I knew it could possibly take decades for us to heal, but I was determined not to inhibit our healing in any way. Not now. I wouldn't allow my own desires to bring another layer of pain to our family.

I continued with therapy and talked with those in my circle. I tried to share my love and devotion for my boys in meaningful ways. I pulled the reigns in a bit, and centered my focus. Though I knew it was important for mommies (and daddies) to recharge and be healthy in order to give their kids what they truly need, I also knew that balance is key. Only then, could we move forward and enjoy our lives, as we should. And slowly, something did happen: the mosaic that was and is "us" began to take shape from that broken glass on the floor; and little by little, Graden, Joel and I began to trust life and experience happiness again.

The Great Waify Boob Conspiracy

"Do cosmetic surgeons know how to do the "waif" look? I want to be waify. I don't want gigantic stripper boobs."

The Long Beach rendezvous with Antonio was in the rearview, and the weeks plodded along peacefully for Graden and me in Orange County. I started to get back on track to building the future I wanted for us. Part of that was to put together a quick moving plan. There were a few important things to accomplish before we could move to Los Angeles.

First, I needed to find a way to start networking again without compromising the happiness or peace at home. I needed to balance my life: no more overnights in LA unless absolutely necessary, but networking was definitely important.

The second priority was Graden's schooling in Los Angeles. His life had been a whirlwind of confusion and pain, especially lately. His daddy had moved away, and his pre-school end-of-year show was attended by me, Joel and a neighborhood friend. Graden grinned and bore it, but I knew he was devastated by his daddy's absence, and my heart was breaking for the little boy who couldn't possibly understand.

I determined I would not subject him to something new unless it could be a very positive experience. I planned to ask Antonio's advice. He was a serious dad with goals for his son to attend college. I also planned to do some of my own homework.

Finally, I knew it was imperative for me to investigate some cosmetic changes to my body (what I *wanted* to look like, vs. what was possible, and who on earth could accomplish it). If I was going to get back in the game, as it were, I had NO intention of looking droopy or saggy. But now that I'd finally shed all of my baby weight, I was one big mess. I felt like a human Shar Pei. I knew that once those *items* were underway, I could zero in on my Los Angeles move and hopefully our new life as a family would begin to fall into place.

The networking thing was easy. I began to accept only those invitations in LA that I determined would be profitable in some way and made the most of what was available to me. I discovered I was pretty damn good at effective time.

At one such event, my gal-pal, Britt applauded me. "Wow! You really know how to pick 'em!" My girlfriend was in awe, as we scampered off to the ladies room.

"What do you mean?" I asked.

"Well," she smiled, "I would have never even *thought* to talk to that guy. He was over at the bar, kind of by himself. He's not real attractive, he looks older, a little overweight, and kind of stuffy. But you went straight for him, and here he ends up being a big VP of Development or whatever at Universal! How did you know to go talk to him?"

"Well," I began tentatively, "The other guys, who were hot, kept looking over my shoulder, as if they would miss a bigger, better deal by talking to me. They weren't even listening to what I was saying. Plus, they had nothing really interesting to say themselves, so I decided to look around for others who might have something more going on, *and*," I added, "who might take *me* seriously."

It was true. We'd been at this party that her network, E! Entertainment Television, had invited us to for just a few minutes, and all the usual suspects were there: the hot soap-opera guys and girls, the agents and managers, the sitcom princesses, TV hosts, etc.

But I soon found my patience for insecure starlets and attention mongers had worn thin. The very thing they craved, adoration and uninterrupted attention, made me want to do just the opposite. So I branched out to the not-so-obvious players around the bar. I knew that appearances could be deceptive, and that I may never know what was *really* going on with that overweight, aging, balding executive in the corner. Marcus, who worked in new car sales for years before we met, always told me that the mistake most unsuccessful sales people made was to *pre-qualify* people. He said some of the wealthiest people would come into the dealership wearing wrinkled khaki shorts and tee-shirts, and pay cash for their brand new cars, while the guys dressed in the three-thousand dollar suits were often stretched so thin they were bad credit risks. For all I knew, my chubby executive friend was a billionaire.

I also thought there was a chance he could relate to me on some level. Here I was, Saggy-Mc-Sagglestein (even though I could hide it with the right wardrobe), hanging with my off-the-charts gorgeous friend. I knew I had a lot to offer, though I may not appear so, so why wouldn't he also have a lot to offer? And I *had* to believe he might see my potential, too.

I determined that I *would* be taken seriously as a viable professional, whether as a producer, writer or whatever I chose to be. That was for certain. As it was, I felt I was joining this game late in life, in my mid-thirties—which made my time even more precious. I had to make every single networking moment count, and pandering after gorgeous celebs-*du-jour* would be an enormous waste of time.

I felt confident about choosing a school for Graden. Its influence on our move was absolute: if we couldn't find the right school, the move was off. But I'd been a mom now for some time. Choosing schools is part of the job.

I talked with Antonio about it and he was a huge advocate for his son's charter school, as well as for the school's residential area, where his ex-wife and son lived. I did some Internet research about grades, graduation rates and sports activities for nearby high schools and talked to other friends in Los Angeles. Many were in favor of private education, but part of my reasoning for the move from Orange County in the first place— aside from the fact that all of my single adult friends were in Los Angeles, as was the business I wanted to work in—was for the culture that Los Angeles offered. I felt that placing Graden in a gilded, guarded private school might defeat that very purpose.

Graden and I took our own personal field trip and visited said charter school. We also started heading up to Los Angeles on Saturdays or Sundays. We would go to the beach or a nearby attraction, and then drive around various neighborhoods, taking note of those we liked. In the end, I went with Antonio's suggestion, combined with my own short list of living arrangement requirements to begin my search. In my mind it was a no-brainer. Graden had already met Antonio's son and they'd had some play dates, and we both really liked the school when we visited. That was the school for him. Great school, built-in friend and fantastic neighborhood.

As for the cosmetic adjustments to my body? Well, that was another story. I had no idea where to begin. I could network my way around a convention of blind, deaf and mute geeks and still come out with some excellent business connections, but ask me back then about plastic surgery, and I was a train wreck waiting to happen. All I knew was what I did *not* want: giant "gozangas" or stripper boobs.

In LA, everyone has a cosmetic surgeon. It's expected. It's like having an eye doctor or dentist. Angelinos don't think of cosmetic surgery as a luxury. They like to think of it as a cost of doing business, or an investment in their career. And trust me: they all have careers that justify cosmetic surgery. I'm not knocking it by *any* means. I became a patient myself, and I would do it again in a New York minute.

I had plenty of referrals from my circle of Los Angeles friends. So, my investigation began. A friend I'd met while volunteering for one of the Screen Actor's Guild strikes told me of a cosmetic surgeon friend of his. Another bartender friend referred me to her favorite. A gal pal recommended one. I learned how to maneuver my way around a consultation very quickly by asking all the right questions. My main concerns were my breasts and my C-section area, which seemed to have organized their *own* unions and strikes.

I knew the surgeon for me had to be located in Los Angeles, as I wanted to have the surgery after moving there. I tried to combine my doctor's consultations with other parties and events in L.A., whenever possible, so I wouldn't waste the gas or a trip. At one such party, I met my old friend and maid of honor, Adrienne Maloof, who had been an LA resident for some time (long before her role as one of the Beverly Hills Housewives). We'd recently reconnected and at this event, she introduced me to her then new fiancé, Dr. Paul Nassif.

I don't believe it was a coincidence that Dr. Nassif happened to be a board-certified cosmetic surgeon in Beverly Hills. Paul encouraged me to come in and meet with his colleague, Dr. Robert Rey (known later for the show "Dr. 90210." Yes. THAT doctor). Dr. Rey did everything below the neck for Dr. Nassif's patients, as Paul's specialty was anything from the neck up. Sounds pretty funny to say it that way—but they really do talk "shop" like it's an *auto body* shop. They'll say things like, "Yeah, Dr. So-and-So does really great body work. I saw a breast aug he did late last week. It was incredible."

Through the arduous process of meeting with cosmetic surgeons, telling them what I wanted and then listening to what was actually possible, I discovered something. It's hard to find a cosmetic surgeon who is *willing* to put small boobs on a gal. Many told me that a large percentage of women who get breast lifts or augmentations, wish they'd gone bigger in size afterward.

I'm different. I know exactly what I like. I had biggish breasts prior to my kids. Those kids sucked it outta me and left me with empty flaps. I know, gross. But my flaps currently fit nicely into a B cup, maybe C on a good day, and I *liked* them that way. I felt thin and pretty. Having large breasts, as I did throughout high school, was very limiting. I felt they made me look bigger than I was. In my mind, smaller boobs would open up a whole new world for me. Never more would I be restricted to wearing button-down blouses a size too big to accommodate my boobs.

When I told surgeons I wanted to keep my bra size and just make what I had look pretty, they did not compute. I tried my little phrase, "I want to look like a waif. Like a ballerina, with small, perky breasts." But no. No comprende. It wasn't that small perky breasts were unheard of. It was simply that in my case, to do it would mean massive scars from cutting away butt loads of skin. So I sighed in disappointment as I listened to each surgeon explain the options available to me, and they varied a bit.

After dragging my ass up to LA for an untold number of consultations and reviewing countless before-and-after photos from various renowned surgeons, I went with the most familiar, who was soon to be Adrienne's husband's "body surgeon." I trusted him and knew that at the very least for Adrienne's sake (and I suppose his, since aside from being a patient, I was also standing in their wedding as a bridesmaid), he'd make sure I looked great. Dr. Rey explained that he could minimize the scars, but he would be limited in how small in breast size he could go. We finally landed on a couple of different sizes and he agreed to allow my best friend Britt into the surgery room while I was under the knife to choose between the two different sizes. We all agreed to leave it up to her to make the final decision, since Britt knew me and my wishes best.

It wasn't until after my surgery that Britt told the hilarious tale of being dressed in scrubs and mask to be ushered toward what she *thought* was going to be two implants on a table, one big, one small, for her to choose from. Instead, she was brought into the operating room to see me in all my gory glory, breasts cut, with sample implants stuffed in. She was horrified! I was lucky she didn't faint at the sight of all the blood. I said to her in disbelief, "Don't you think *I* saw the implants on the table? We needed to see what they would look like on *me*!" We cracked up over THAT one!

She said, "Yeah! They took me in there and I was so shocked! I was trying to remember what you said about wanting to be waify, and here on one side was this giant basketball boob, and on the other side was a smaller, but certainly not waify boob! I told them I was inclined to go with the smaller and they actually tried to talk me out of it!

"It was a like a conspiracy. They said, 'Let's take a vote. Who in here thinks the bigger size will look better?' and Lisa, *every-one-in-that-room* raised their hand. They were *all* against me! It was so hard!

"But I had to keep going back to what you said. 'Pick the one that is closest to waif,' so that's what I did!"

It wasn't long before Dr. Rey abandoned the practice of allowing friends or family members into surgery to choose between sizes. Yes, we can now add "changes the way men do business" to my resume.

During my whole interaction with Dr. Nassif's practice, I learned that it's pretty common for those who choose to have a little nip-tuck here and there, to also have the tendency to become addicted to plastic surgery procedures. The people there discussed this issue with me because, well, I ended up buying the whole shebang in one fell swoop. I suppose the cosmetic surgeons have to do this full disclosure thing because their surgeries are mostly elective. Insurance does not pay or regulate cosmetic procedures. When I began to say yes to everything, they must have thought the "new me" would be sucked in.

I didn't sign up to have a complete overhaul in one or even two or three meetings. You have to remember, I was also friends with Adrienne and socialized with her and Paul regularly. I was at Adrienne's place touching up my makeup just before we were going out on one such evening, and my post-divorce saggy eyelids and dark circles, which no concealer could cover up, were giving me trouble. So I asked Paul about it. He took me under a light and examined my eyes, and said, "I can help you. Come in to see me when you see Dr. Rey and we'll figure it out."

So I did. I signed up to have Dr. Nassif fix my saggy-droopy skin on my upper eyelids, something I later learned I inherited from Mommy dear. To help remove the dark hollow circles under my eyes, Dr. Nassif planned to do a fat repositioning technique. I enlisted Dr. Rey to overhaul my breasts, remove the excess skin around my vertical C-section scar, and in the process, repair a hernia that was another little present from carrying Graden those nine months. Huh, it kind of does remind me of when I take my car in!

As the months fast-forwarded to weeks before our big move to Los Angeles, our excitement grew. Graden and I found a huge, lovely two-bedroom condo just a half block from his new school and I began to pick up work marketing for another area physician (a colleague and friend of Dr. Nassif's). I also began to reestablish the Los Angeles connections I'd made at the Kentucky Derby. Come hell or high water or both, I would work in television and this was my grand opportunity. Finally! No one I was married or connected to was in a position to tell me "No. I don't want to live in L.A." or "No, you shouldn't take that job."

Let's Get This Party Started

"I need an angel, Lisa. Can you work for me in Vegas? I'm doing a little show for the Billboard Music Awards." —Aaron Anderson

I remember where I was the moment I heard of the first tower falling.

Just before our move to Los Angeles, I quit my corporate job and took on any other work I could get. I found a couple of part-time jobs. One of them was with a Hollywood event company, which I landed through a friend of Adrienne Maloof's, because I thought it could open doors to meet more industry people. The other was at Gap Kids & Baby Gap in Beverly Hills—discounts on kids' clothes, people! We were still awaiting approval for Graden to attend his new school in LA prior to our move, so he and his nanny were at home in Orange County on the morning of September 11, 2001.

I'd spent the night at a friend's in Los Angeles so I could be on time for the early shift at Baby Gap. I was driving in to work on the 101 Freeway when I heard radio personalities Jamie White and Danny Bonaduce freaking out about the first tower. I thought it was another one of the sick jokes they were known for. When I arrived at work, the few of us who made it in got word from the corporate office that all Gap stores would close for the day.

A co-worker and I popped over the Beverly Hilton lobby to watch the coverage. I called Graden's babysitter and told her to bring him with her to the hotel. No one was sure at that time of anyone's safety in *any* city, so I wasn't taking any chances. The news reporters speculated that if San Onofre's nuclear power plant, south of Orange County, was targeted, all of Southern California could be taken out.

My thoughts? "If we are going down, my little one and I will be together." Joel was at his friend's parent's house and couldn't get to me, so I asked him to stay put.

It turned out that the Latin Grammys were taking place that very week at the Beverly Hilton, so the hotel was packed with Latin American Music celebrities. Here I was right in the middle of the epitome of networking heaven, but I had no desire to do so, nor would it be appropriate. I met some folks who would impact my life in ways I couldn't imagine at the time, but it was an extremely frightening and paralyzing period for everyone.

Just a little over a month later, while our nation's wounds were still raw, futures uncertain and the streets of Los Angeles eerily vacant, Graden, his live-in nanny and I made the official move to LA. I hired the nanny to help out while I networked my way around the film and television industry as we settled into our new home, neighborhood and life. Yes, a live-in nanny. A strict resolution I made after my divorce was to never again be the single mom who couldn't make a last-minute trip or meeting because I was without a sitter. I refused to limit my possibilities because I was single—again.

It wasn't that I was wealthy. As a matter of fact, I'd given up my job and all sense of security to move to Los Angeles. On paper, the move, let alone a live-in nanny, looked insane. Not a few of my friends and neighbors in Orange County made sure I knew they thought so. Of course, now I have the benefit of hindsight and the proof of my successes to be able to tell my critics from back then to, well, suck it. Some could say I was "lucky," but I love how life and karma snap back around like a whip and remind people of themselves and the things they say and do, myself included. What many did *not* know was that my settlement in the divorce made paying the nanny for the first six months no problem. After that it was going to be up to me. True to form, I was willing to gamble I'd be okay after six months.

Besides, I had all kinds of tricks for making things work as a single mom, economically, socially and logistically. I had a checklist I used for years reminding me of essentials I always needed:

- lists of babysitters referred by the local area church and private high school
- the names and phone numbers of Graden's school friends for play dates and more
- a bag full of toiletries, jammies, school supplies, *Underoos*, socks and tooth brush in the trunk of my car for Graden—it's what I moved on to after the diaper bag phase
- a bag for myself I fondly referred to as my "just in case," containing important toiletries, perfume, sexy underwear/lingerie, an extra pair of shoes, lip gloss, hair products and anything else I thought of along the way.

I have always tried to surround myself with resources for every situation.

I recall our move-in day very clearly. My ex-husband Marcus came out from New Mexico for a few days to help. The dust had settled from his major meltdown and he had some big-ticket items to claim from our existing home, so he was very amenable to helping with the move. I suppose he came mostly to get his personal belongings, but he also took the opportunity to try to reconnect with his son and.... wait for it... with me!

The Marcus-style attempt at reconnecting with me was, well... oh so *Marcus*. It was sort of a half-yawn, "I'm-not-really-sure-I-want-to-do-this-anyway, but-what-do-you-think?" approach. Not that his style mattered. The nightmares I'd experienced with him were etched on my brain and branded on my heart. There was no chance in hell I would go back. He could have ridden in on a saddled unicorn accompanied by the LA Philharmonic, with first class tickets to Europe... and the answer still would have been the same: "What? Are you FRIGGIN' KIDDING me?"

Regardless of this, he was surprisingly helpful. I was happy to receive his assistance nonetheless, especially considering that the week after the move, I was to undergo my cosmetic surgery. How "LA" is that?

My strategic plan after the move was simple:

1) Get in.

2) Get fixed up.

3) Get busy.

And that is what I did.

The next day, I went in for surgery while the nanny and Marcus handled Graden and the unpacking and organization of some three hundred and fifty-plus boxes stacked in our new condo. Pretty sweet, huh? No. Really. I mean it in the total frat boy sense of the word, as in "SUHHH-WEEEET!!" I was pretty happy about the help, to say the least.

Once I was up and around, I began making calls and did everything possible to reconnect with the production folks I'd met at the Kentucky Derby. I think I called Aaron, the producer, about fifty times over the course of the next month. This was before email was so prevalent, much less *any* social media platform like Facebook or Twitter.

I remember being so incredibly determined in those fervent days to make something happen out of nothing. I would catch Aaron live and on the phone and sell myself like I was the best thing since sliced bread—and hey, to me I was. I told him about my producing background on the news (for about, um, two whole months as a temp) and how I was a floor director during the newscast at the little affiliate station in Albuquerque (once, I think), as well as teleprompter operator (that part was true and it was my main responsibility), even my time as News Desk Assistant, scanning the radios for breaking news. I mentioned all of my time working with celebrities who came to New Mexico, *like…you know…the famous Franklin Graham? You know, Billy's son?* He came to our church and we got to know him pretty well, I told Aaron. I bragged about the major events I'd managed (also true). The point was, I *knew* I could do this and it's what I wanted. That was enough for me, so it was *going* to be enough for him. He just didn't know it yet.

As the weeks went by and I met people at events here and there, I collected business cards—yes, those little rectangular things— so I could maintain contact with many of them via email and phone while remaining conscientious about being available for Graden now that we were living in LA. My business card file grew exponentially in a matter of weeks. I filed the cards by topic: cameraman on fill-in-the-blank show, producer of films, actor. Anyone who was connected at all to the entertainment industry made the cut, and I would try to make "something out of nothing" with each of them.

I wanted work, people! W-O-R-K – work.

In retrospect, I learned something during these months as a freshling in Los Angeles: *most* people move to Southern California to pursue their dreams in the entertainment industry and most try to make something out of nothing. I was no exception.

For the most part, what I got from these early meetings were a bunch of connections to other people also networking hopefully, and a whole lot of people wanting my marketing and PR help—people with no money and a lot of need. It took me some time, but I eventually learned that to give away my time and expertise was, well, a waste of my time and expertise. So that stopped pretty damn quick—like, after a couple of months. Okay, years. I've always been a bit thick in the head and a sucker for a fun project that doesn't pay me what it should.

Somewhere in the midst of all of this, I booked an event for the event company I worked for. I got the gig through Antonio, who was shooting a DVD for Marilyn Manson. My job: the celebrity after-party. I had to stock their back-lot party tent with booze and provide the organization and staff. This I did. As the party grew packed and the bar backlogged, I grabbed a tray and went into the celebrity VIP area to take drink orders. I served drinks to Nicolas Cage and Lisa Marie Presley (they were engaged at the time) and Nicolas' son (who was a big fan). I served Marilyn and a slew of other celebrities. The best part for me was I was able to give tickets to my son Joel and his then-girlfriend, who were huge fans.

This was no venue for me to convince people to put me to work on their television production, but the production manager of the project and I became friends, and in the next couple of years, she referred me for work on a few occasions. It was definitely a good gig to land, but I still had the ache to get "in" on an actual television production. My determination to make it happen, and my thirst to succeed only deepened after working on that event.

I was still hanging with some of the glam-squad in Tinsel Town, including Adrienne Maloof, her fiancé Dr. Nassif and many of their friends. I was spending plenty of time with one of my besties Britt and my new Hollywood television industry friends. Britt and I were even talking about throwing a holiday party. There was no shortage of entertainment types to rub shoulders with, but none were offering jobs—not the kind I wanted, anyway. I never gave up finding any excuse to connect with Aaron and of course there was still Antonio, another person who was connected to Aaron.

That relationship had its own funny side: the minute I made the move up to Los Angeles, Antonio decided it was time to put things to rest between us and take another shot at a relationship with his former girlfriend. It *never fails. The second my situation becomes more convenient, the guy comes up with an iron-clad excuse.* Sound familiar? Anyone? It seemed the story of my life, but I wasn't going to let that deter me or get in the way of my goals. I worked at getting a job in the industry from every possible angle and that included reaching out to Antonio.

Then one day toward the end of November, after umpteen pesky calls and repeated messages to Aaron, I received a phone call from him.

"I need an angel, Lisa. Are you available?" he said.

I could barely contain my girlish squeals before I said in the most casual and nonchalant tone I could muster: "Sure. What do you have in mind?"

"It's for this little show I am doing in Vegas for the people at Fox," He continued, "It's the pre-show for the Billboard Music Awards. We're calling it the Billboard Bash."

I wanted so badly to shout out loud at him, "ARE YOU FREAKING KIDDING ME? HELLO! THIS IS WHAT I'VE BEEN WAITING FOR!" But I managed to eek out, "What are the dates again?" then, "I think I can make it work!" in a surprisingly calm and professional manner.

Once I was on board, and was given the "call time" for my first day, I felt an enormous sense of accomplishment and a sense of deep satisfaction wash over me. I wasn't an idiot. I knew this was only one job and I still had no idea what would come after that, but I felt like this was the break into the industry I'd dreamed of. After the past few years and the desperate times, it felt extremely gratifying.

I soon learned what Aaron meant by "angel" was that he needed a replacement for his regular assistant, who had fallen ill. Aaron was in a bind for this upcoming show. It wasn't that I wished ill of anyone, certainly, but I was definitely doing the "lucky me" dance that day.

"Call times" in the film and television industry are the times and dates given to cast and crew for their expected arrival on set. I was virginal when I showed up my first day. I'll never forget: In preparation for working on the Billboard Bash, I joined Aaron on set at the Shrine Auditorium in downtown Los Angeles where another of his projects was underway, pre-production for an award show for VH-1 called "My VH-1 Music Awards"—sort of a People's Choice Awards for music. The awards were taking place on December 2, 2001, the same weekend we were to be in Vegas prepping for the Billboard Bash, which would take place on the eve of the Billboard Music Awards on December 4. Apparently, Aaron had enough clout to work for VH-1 prior to the Vegas show, and leave in time for the Billboard Bash. I learned this, too, was reason he needed me, as much of his team, many of whom I recognized from the Mint Jubilee, would be tied up working on the VH-1 show.

The production office was electric with activity. I was so thrilled to be there, they could have said, "You're on trash duty, Lisa," and I would have enthusiastically grabbed a garbage bag and gone to work. Nothing was beneath me.

Turned out Aaron and his team were responsible for what's called talent logistics. This means the MTV or VH-1 full-time staff would book "talent," or musical artists to perform or attend the show, and Aaron's team, also referred to as "freelancers," worked the logistics: handling the talent from the booking onward, including credentials, travel, transportation, accommodations, dressing room requests—basically anything to be coordinated for any given show. We also assisted with talent "wrangling" during the show. This meant making sure celebrities were in their expected spot on cue throughout the show: backstage to go on, in their seat to be "caught on camera," or whatever.

Regardless, this was production and I'd learned in Albuquerque that no production depends on just one person. Everybody plays a vital role. I learned that while I maneuvered the satellite dish in the bitter cold, atop our news crew van at the International Balloon Fiesta in Albuquerque at five in the morning, or as I stood in for the floor director way before my time, because I was good at my job. The trash collectors, producers, talent coordinators, credentials managers, staging, lighting and sound, you name it—they're all vital. The jobs are also fairly consistent from city to city, no matter the type of programming. I learned that much of the terminology and the people the industry attracts are pretty consistent as well.

Though there were many similarities, there is one thing that differentiated this kind of production from those in New Mexico: we were in Hollywood, people! *Hellllo!* Everyone here was literally *thrilled* to be on the show, working and getting paid to do what they loved. In Albuquerque, people had a general sense of pride over their work and loved what they did, but the newsroom was one of the most negatively charged, stressful, toxic environments I'd ever experienced. It was tough to feel as though your future was bright in that space. Here, I seriously could feel the excitement and positive energy and I was ready to drink in every ounce I could get. For goddsakes, the Craft Service person, the person in charge of snacks in production—SNACKS!—walked around throughout the day offering mini iced-cappuccinos, quesadilla bites hot off the grill and various other delights. Compared to the Doritos, M&Ms and Snickers bars I would soon see on other sets, this was elaborate. I'd never seen any production quite like this, and I soon learned that MTV and VH-1 had a pretty good reputation for treating their teams well.

Although I was a newbie to the world of being officially employed in the entertainment industry, I didn't go in totally blind. I also had the benefit of Britt, who'd been working professionally in the business for years and was happy to clue me in when I was curious.

One of the fondest memories I have of that first day was of Aaron and me sitting down to work in the VH-1 production offices at the Shrine. I went straight into production mode, undeterred and un-intimidated. If Aaron needed a contact name or phone number for someone important, without his asking, I got on the phone, posed as someone else when necessary and got him the info. When he needed to figure out which artists were *not* performing but would be attending the Billboard Music Awards (so we could build our show), I made a few calls. Once connected, I assured the award show's producer we would not be irresponsible with the information and had a list faxed over immediately.

This kind of activity went on for some time when I met Mick. While Aaron generally was the head-honcho on the MTV side of productions, his protégé Mick was the substitute "Aaron" on the VH-1 side, but they worked together on many shows. He half-whispered to Aaron, "She's good." I smiled. Now all I needed to do was figure out how to stay on this team for future shows.

Aside from those few days at the Shrine and a couple of meetings over at Fox Studios to discuss particulars of the event, we pushed forward to "Day of Show." For this event, we were the entire talent department, answering only to the execs at Fox. Our show was to be the pre-party to the actual awards show, and our entire team would also have tickets to the awards show (just another perk).

I loved every minute working as Aaron's right hand. When the day came that Aaron, a whole other set of production people (his B-team, I gathered, since his A-team was working the VH-1 show) and I arrived at the MGM grand to begin prepping our show. I was in heaven. Not only was I pursuing my dreams, I was surrounded once again by incredible people.

And Aaron was freaking HILARIOUS. We enjoyed every single day (well, I can only speak for myself, and it ROCKED) and the days tend to be extremely long in television production. Typical call times for the Billboard Bash were 7:00 AM at the latest, and we generally worked through and didn't "wrap" until about 6:30 PM without any real breaks. That's what Craft Service is for and why so many people like me ended up bringing in yogurt, carrots and string cheese to combat the fatty trail mix, chips, salsa and quesadillas at a regular Craft Service table.

Before I go on, there is something to note about production people: like everyone else, they are either sober, or they like to drink, sometimes a LOT. I fell into the latter category in that I did not abstain from alcohol (and it's still true today). I didn't go crazy and drink during work, or every night out by any means, but I definitely liked my Fridays. I would have a single cocktail on school nights once in a while as well.

I'd had my fill of living sober with Marcus. Those days were behind me. It didn't mean I went nuts all the time, or that I was stupid and got behind the wheel—*ever*—but I enjoyed myself. Period. After each long day in Vegas trolling the lists of artists coming to town, inviting them to perform or attend red carpet, and other various talent logistics, we were ready to have drinks somewhere in the MGM.

And that we did.

Aaron informed us at one point that he needed to hire someone who, as on the Miss America pageant, would announce the artists and celebrities walking the red carpet and interview them briefly just before they entered our show's venue. I was thrilled to be able to suggest that Britt come on as our Red Carpet hostess, and Aaron went for it. Unfortunately, Britt didn't know the names or projects of popular music acts in the least. Ask her about any actor or other celebrity, and she could rattle off all the details, but Top 40 music? Uh, no. I remember running up to her ahead of certain acts to tell her, "These are the guys from Incubus," or "this is Aaron Carter. His brother, Nick, is a Backstreet Boy." In other moments, I'd be waiting for one of the celebrities to finish being interviewed in the line, and I would see Britt waving me down out of the corner of my eye. I'd run over and she'd say "Who are these guys over here? I have no idea what to say about them!" It was fun to have a chance to *clue her in on* some things for a change.

Incubus ended up performing their new hit, *Drive,* among other tunes. Aaron Carter also performed. I'm sure it's documented somewhere but I can't seem to recall the rest.

I do know this: Aaron, being a brilliant visionary, kept coming up with incredible ideas that had to be approved by the producers of the main Billboard Music Awards show—they couldn't let our show be too similar to or more spectacular than theirs. I'm not sure if it was this particular event or one soon after when Aaron wanted to have the artist Pink perform her hit of the day, "Get this Party Started." He suggested, in front of me, that we have her pop out of a cake onstage. It was brilliant and was very quickly vetoed.

When that very song with the cake and all surfaced during the main show, I remember saying to Aaron, "Heyyyy, they used your idea." I couldn't fathom at the time his disappointment. I thought if I'd been in his situation then, I would have been proud they used the idea, and content knowing that every time I saw those producers, *they* knew and I knew they snagged and took credit for my idea. Knowing me, I would have mentioned it to them with a wink "Hey, nice bit with Pink and the cake the other night!" What I learned later after much interaction with producers and creative types in the business, particularly those in a position to use and take credit for ideas other than their own, was that it was sort of like the kiss of death from the Godfather when they did this to you, in terms of working with them. Why? Think about it. You could withhold good ideas in the future, go behind their back to get your ideas approved and outshine them. You could get even in any number of other ways if they continued to work with you. But also, if they stole your ideas, they *had* to know they were being small-minded, small emotionally, and generally lame, creatively. Sadly, instead of later pulling you aside and apologizing or making "good" in other ways, they stop working with you. They usually can't handle facing the victim. So, I guess Aaron was thinking he might be challenged, at best, to ever work with them again.

Despite the usual politics and stress in production, Aaron and I very quickly developed a hilarious repartee we later called the "Radio Show," replete with "listeners" who would be "so disappointed" if we didn't have our daily banter or shtick. Add to that a few strategic cocktails and we logged a gaggle of hilarious "radio shows," that's for damn sure. As the months passed, we would get on the phone and dish on the events of the production from the night or week before. No one was safe, certainly not the celebrities in attendance.

In Vegas for the Billboard Bash, I learned that Aaron always brought a posse with him to every show. It always surprised me, the number of people who were willing to fly in, drive hundreds or thousands of miles and put themselves up in hotels, for the promise of tickets to televised awards shows or the possibility of attending the after-party.

Posse attendees at the Billboard Bash consisted of a potential business partner of Aaron's, Kevin; Kevin's friend Alan (whom we soon learned was the money behind the venture); and their limo driver Matt. Yep, you read that right: We had access to a limo, and all that entails. Weeeeeee! We definitely utilized our "car service" on that trip.

Once our Pre-Billboard Music Awards production was finished, we partied it up at the MGM Grand. Betty Boop, as in one of the lobby bars at MGM, took on a whole new meaning. I remember Aaron thought I may like to get to know his potential business partner Kevin, and though he wasn't a bad-looking guy, I wasn't so sure. I was a spitfire during that time (not that I'm not now, come to think of it), with so much energy I pretty much outlasted everyone on the production.

Everyone except Kevin, apparently, who found me while I was looking to meet up with any remaining production crew. I ran into him alone in the crew's favorite lounge. We began to talk, and Kevin was quite a talker. He went on and on about his beliefs on life, and what he was looking for, and pretty quickly I understood he was giving me not only his dating schtick, but was trying to convey what was going on in his mind.

The problem was, I didn't really *want* to know what was in there. I was enjoying playing, fluttering about and drinking in every ounce of awesome-sauce that life had to offer. This guy just kept going on and on about his thoughts and philosophies—it bored me to tears! If only I could recall the details of his musings, but basically this guy was all over the map and couldn't seem to make a single point.

It got so I couldn't shut him up. My eyes glazed over. He still didn't get it. I started to yawn and drift off. No dice. Yap yap yap yap yap.

Finally the moment came when I was able to excuse myself from Mr. Philosophizer. I let Aaron know he was definitely *not* for me. It wasn't that annoying, because I knew this guy's type and how to handle him. He had the "Oooo Pretty" thing goin' on. Though he could ramble on forever about nothing, pretty objects, if cleverly utilized, could easily distract him.

From there on out, anytime Mr. Philosopher came near, I'd say things like "Oh my God, Kevin, look at that hot cabaret dancer!" or "Don't you love those heels on her! You should go for it!" It was Vegas! There was a plethora of distractions to "ooo and ahhh" him with.

Aaron found the whole concept hilarious. He would later laugh about it and tell others about my escapades, "Lisa was sneaking around the casino trying to ditch Kevin. Then she would dangle pretty little things in front of him if he ever caught her to distract him!" It took some skill too, especially when factoring in other hot guys I wanted to talk to. Kevin had no filter. He would walk up and start talking, sending every single guy running from boredom. Throughout the rest of our trip, I was forced to employ my best ninja disappearing tricks to keep him at bay.

The next day was all about meetings where Alan, Kevin and Aaron planned the launch of their production company. I don't know how or why I was included. Aaron was and is like that. He loves to bring along his friends and allow them to experience his world. I know that now, but back then, I was just glad not to be asked to leave. Listening in, mostly to Alan and Aaron, was intriguing. Kevin would pontificate for moments when he could, but it was interesting to watch, nonetheless.

That evening was the actual awards show. We had tickets and were able to see music's brightest stars like Alicia Keys up close and personal as they ascended the stage to accept awards. This was the year of Alicia's now infamous breakout album *Songs in A Minor*. It was the very album her original label, Arista Records asked her to make changes to (after ousting Clive Davis, the man who'd signed Alicia). Clive went off and started J Records, brought Alicia over, allowed her to make the album the way she wanted and the rest is history. Her album cleaned up at the awards shows that year and it must have been really gratifying. I know I loved the album. I also loved learning the inside stories about these artists from Aaron and others I worked with.

Being at this show with our all-access production credentials was pretty awesome. To be there and not have to work was even better.

Once the show was over, we all convened at the limo pick up to PAR-TAY, which calls to mind another fantastic memory. Wherever we went—Hard Rock, Bellagio, wherever we wanted to go—we arrived in style. As the evening progressed and our alcohol consumption continued, every one of us became divas. If we'd call our limo driver to say we were heading down to the pick up area, and the limo was not there when we arrived, Aaron would jokingly whine, "Lisa! Where's my fucking limo? I just want my limo to be here when it's supposed to be, dammit! Is that too much to ask?"

What a fantastic foray into television production it was for me. I knew it was only the beginning of a brand new grand adventure. I couldn't wait to get home and tell Graden all about it (tales of cocktails and other adult situations excluded, of course).

My Son The Homeless Guy

"Are you sure ma'am? A lot of people in L.A. like to protect the homeless." —LA police officer

The extraordinary deflation that occurs after wrapping a production (especially those highly charged events involving A-list celebrities and live performances like the Billboard Bash and Billboard Music Awards) are like hangovers. You're flying high and everything is a bit of a blur, then you go to sleep and awaken to a keen sense of nothing and maybe a little pain.

Then again, I wouldn't really know about the hangover part, because I don't get hangovers. I know. Hate me now and be done with it.

But the morning after wrapping a production it's just sheer, utter silence. No phones ringing, no urgent cries on the headset for someone to get Ben Affleck to the stage. No, it's just you, your bed and silence. It takes some getting used to. I always tell people who've planned a huge event or wedding, to imagine doing that every other week and then waking up to just nothing. No new bride. No new home. You get the idea.

When I felt this way after the *Billboard Bash* production, I wasn't even aware that the swift, immediate and forced "lull" between gigs was a regular downside to a production career. I simply thought it was my post-divorce anxiety knocking at the door, so I attacked it head-on as I'd been doing now for months. I got busy pimping myself out for the next gig, making calls, writing emails and anything else I could think of to secure more work in entertainment.

During this time, I also met and befriended Antonio's ex-wife, Sheila. We met on Graden's first day of school, just after 9-11. Before our October move to LA, we commuted daily for two hours so he could start the year with his class.

As we were walking in to find his classroom, heading straight for us on the sidewalk ahead was Antonio's son, whom Graden had already befriended on recent play dates.

"Hi, Graden!" he said happily.

Graden returned an enthusiastic hello, while I noticed this beautiful blonde woman who looked like Michelle Pfeiffer next to him. This *is Antonio's EX? $%@#**&%!* I thought.

She was a gorgeous blonde and spoke with a beautifully sophisitcated British accent. Antonio had told me all about her (a choreographer born in England, lived in Paris, traveled the world with her dancers. She and Antonio met in Japan), but I had no idea what to expect. She was stunning. It brought up some interesting emotions in me. Antonio's and my consensual split was still fresh. As progressive as I believed the new me to be about my newly single status, I must admit there was a certain sting to the end of my fun and games with Antonio.

I'm one to definitely enjoy my fun, and I do not like it to end. I also do not like being told no. There is no "no" in my "where there is a will, there is a way" world. I'm even more difficult about it when someone else has to abandon our "fun" and move on. Just seeing this lovely lady aroused that sting of rejection and started me comparing myself to her in every way.

So, I hauled off and clocked her.

K*idding!* I *befriended* her. The truth is, she was a doll and it was only about two minutes before Sheila's personality melted any insecurity away.

I mentioned quickly how I'd worked with Antonio and we'd gotten the boys together for a couple of play dates, and she was very sweet. We chatted for a bit and when she learned of my predicament of commuting every day, she offered to let Graden and me to stay at her place any time we needed.

Sheila also agreed to have Graden for a sleep-over during my holiday party with Britt, although she herself was unable to make it. That's one of the things I love about LA. I kept running into people who were sweet, friendly, energetic, and generally interested in health and fitness, and above all, happy to live and let live (and I still meet people like that today). I had no idea just how much Antonio's ex-wife knew about our little trysts, but she extended her hand of "single mom friendship" or camaraderie regardless. It spoke volumes to me about not only Sheila and her depth, but about how vital it was to never lose heart about people. Just when you think they've all gone to hell in a hand-basket, their surprising acts of random kindness give you a reason to snap your mouth shut and renew your faith.

About this time, Joel—as I guessed he would—came to his senses, and decided that although he'd given me an unequivocal "no" about moving up to LA while I was conducting my condo search, it was now time to make the move. Wonders never cease, but he wanted to move in with Graden, his nanny and me, into our two-bedroom condo. I simply couldn't accommodate him like I wanted to (and I *really wanted to)*, but he pleaded and negotiated his way onto the couch in my den, and according to him, only until he could find a good job and save up enough for his own place.

Of course, I helped him there. At one of many events, I'd met a music supervisor for motion pictures, as well the A&R rep at Immergent Records. If you've ever heard of an album called *Rumors* by a little band called Fleetwood Mac, it was *that* record label. Said friend needed a runner or "Girl-Friday" sort of assistant, and Joel was their girl… guy. See? All this moving and networking was for my kids! Hey, it is true in a sense. Our new lives ended up benefitting all of us in some very unexpected ways!

During this time, Joel discovered the roof of my condo building. One might believe he'd developed a deep-rooted love for nature and being out under the stars. Yeah, right. I knew it was mostly because he could smoke cigarettes and visit with friends without his mom around. I didn't really understand the roof thing at first, so I went up to investigate one day. I was incensed to find he had a sleeping bag up there, a little propped-up tent sort of contraption, and scattered beer cans and cigarette butts all over the place. I marched down the stairs and read Joel the Riot Act, making him promise to "get his butt up there" at his first opportunity to clean his gigantic mess. It wasn't as if anyone in the building ever went up to the roof. Nothing was up there but air conditioning vents and cement. But it wasn't meant to be a hang-out, let alone a refugee camp.

After the Billboard Bash, the holiday season was coming fast. While pursuing more television gigs and with my incredibly crazy, holiday party-planning life, I seemed to keep forgetting to follow up with Joel about his mess. I'd never had to ask him twice in the past when it came to cleaning things up, so I let it slip my mind. He was just a *clean* kid! But something very funny happened that I'll never forget. Joel refused to believe it when I told him about it. He still doesn't believe it to this day. It is one of my favorite stories to tell about my life in Los Angeles.

I came home one day after walking to Graden's school to pick him up, and as we were entering our building from the front, two police officers were looking at our building's directory, about to buzz someone.

"Can I help you?"

"Yes ma'am. We're responding to a call of a reported homeless person who's been sleeping on the roof."

"Oh!" I said laughingly, "That's not a homeless person. It's my son. I have an eighteen-year-old son (as a January baby, he was close!), and he's been going up there to camp out with his sleeping bag. I told him to clean up his mess, but he must not have gotten to it yet."

There was a little pause as the two officers exchanged quick glances.

"Uh, are you sure ma'am?" he cleared his throat, "Because you don't look old enough to have an eighteen-year-old son and a lot of people, especially around the holidays here in Los Angeles, they are very sensitive and protective over the homeless community. They don't want them to be put out on the street."

Before he could go on I interjected, trying to control laughter, "No, I swear! He really is my son! If you like you can come up to my condo and I'll show you pictures of him. Right, Graden?" I said to my little guy.

"Yep!" he yelped with a grin.

"No, it's okay, if you say so. We'll leave it at that. We just run into this all the time. Thank you for your time."

As I walked up the stairs, I called Joel's cell and left him a message about the entire nutty incident. *Of all the damn people in Los Angeles,* I thought, *this happens to ME.* Once again, I envisioned myself in black-and-white "television land," half-expecting Ricky Ricardo to come out and say "Leeeesa! You know you got yourself into this when you let that kid sleep on the roof in the first place! I don't care how clean he is, he has some esplainin' tah do!"

As I said, Joel wouldn't hear any of it. He was convinced I'd concocted the whole story to get him to stop sleeping on the roof, ending his days of paradise, case of mistaken homeless identity that it was. I can't really blame him, though. It would be just like me to concoct such a story, if only I were that devious—er...brilliant.

In Los Angeles, the holidays are a time when all things go "dark" or shut down in terms of film and television production. Between mid-December and oh, pretty much mid-January in the entertainment industry, production comes to a halt. There is little to no activity and even less work. I planned to attack this lack of activity the only way I knew how: I would book as many nights out as possible to various hot spots in Hollywood, to events, and every other "thing" that would make the clock tick faster while the entertainment industry slept and my little Graden was off visiting his daddy.

Regardless of what *wasn't* happening, I didn't want to be home in my big beautiful condo by myself for several hours every night. Some people think it's a godsend when the kids are away. They just adore the ability to stay in, sip tea, relax and watch uninterrupted movies or television. I get it. I really do. But back then, I'd long since lost track of every television show I had grown fond of while pregnant with and then raising the baby version of Graden, and really couldn't be bothered with it now. I was antsy and didn't have the money to buy new books or to spend on spa treatments. Yep, spa treatments. I would have *totally* indulged in those babies if I'd had the cash, but it wasn't happening in this period in my life. Instead it was get-me-outta-the-house PARTY TIME! It was this mentality that earned me the reputation of being a "party" girl—or "trouble" as Sheila soon came to refer to me.

It was no surprise to anyone when Britt and I planned a fabulous holiday party to celebrate my arrival in Tinsel Town. As the days trucked along, the need to get ROCKING, and fast, became urgent. We planned the party for December 15, 2001. With Graden's school coming to a close for the holidays at the same time, things got feverish.

As Britt and I had both lived in New Mexico, we were familiar with an annual event there called Holiday Olé. We thought it had a good ring to it, and built from there. In a quick brainstorming session, we decided to call our party "Holiday L.A."

Our premise was a "wrap party" for our fake film called "Holiday L.A." We described our "film" as "the story of one girl's dream to move to Los Angeles and pursue a career in the film and television industry." We created invitations, masquerading as a Hollywood production company, Brit-Davis Productions. We included call sheets with the arrival date and time and elicited the help of Aaron and his business partner's limo for the evening. We hired a craft service person and bartender, brought in two bathtubs full of ice, all the booze and food we could think of as well as "set" props: lighting, director's chairs, makeup mirrors, cables and more to provide a convincing backdrop to a wrap party for a film. Our guests were the cast and crewmembers, all with call times. Once we started coming up with ideas, we found the fun and interesting possibilities were limitless.

We invited all the people I'd met at every networking event and job in recent months: the older, stuffy guy from the E! red carpet event, Antonio and his girlfriend (whom I did not shoot, though I toyed with the idea before getting to know her), Aaron and the new production company contingent, as well as some new friends and connections. Britt invited many of her good friends and colleagues as well and called it my "welcome to LA" party.

We secured parking at my son's school a half a block away, and set the limo up to circle around, pick people up and deliver them to my door. Our craft service gal set up her table and made amazing appetizers for her helpers to pass among the crowd.

People were thrilled to cooperate. As they arrived I greeted them at the door, production headset on, frantically proclaiming "You're late! We've got to get you over to makeup right away," and whisk them off to the back of the house for "makeup"—which entailed a quick tour of the place, ending with the master bedroom which had a big production-style makeup mirror on display for the night (but no one actually got any makeup done – something I still to this day wish we'd made happen. How fun would *that* have been?).

Later in the evening, I searched for Aaron. I hadn't forgotten it was his birthday the following day, nor did the fact he was trying to downplay it escape me. He was quite helpful when I found him out back talking with friends and I shrieked, "Aaron! I need your help! We've got a fire!" He ran with me to the front of the condo where everyone was gathered to sing happy birthday to him with a cake that was, yes, on fire.

At one point, a musician friend I'd met through Aaron and I performed a Fiona Apple song.

Yes.

Fiona Apple.

At a holiday party.

It was priceless. Especially since my "friend" was very tipsy by the time we chose to perform, and our song "Shadow Boxer," while meant to be a ballad, turned into somewhat of a dirge. It was more like a funeral march than a nice piece of party entertainment. But despite that, all in all, the party was a tremendous success. I think the last people sauntered out around 3:30 AM. It was so successful, in fact, that Britt and I thought "maybe we should actually make the movie 'Holiday L.A.' since the wrap party went so well!" *Now where to get twenty million dollars? Hmm, maybe one day.*

When the last people trickled out, I hit the pillow like a lead balloon. I think I slept twelve hours that night.

Just before Graden left for New Mexico to be with his dad, we celebrated Christmas. We invited Sheila and her son over for dinner and a playdate. Graden's dad was buying him the newest gaming system that year, so Graden and I discussed getting rid of the old one, and he decided he wanted to give it to Antonio's son. They'd turned into pretty good little buddies since our move, and I worked hard to facilitate their spending time together.

Between our holiday party and the first week of January, while we both were without kids during some of the winter holidays, I made a habit of inviting Sheila to accompany me to hear a new artist perform at the Viper Room or visit some other Hollywood haunt. It was pretty easy when both the boys were gone, as long as I could convince her to get out on a school night, but once they were both back in town, she would say in her British way something like "Cheers, I'd really love to, but I don't have a sitter for my little guy."

I would promptly reply, "Bring him over here! He can sleep over and they'll go to school together in the morning."

One time while we were out, I overheard Sheila speaking to some cute guy at the bar. She played innocent (I knew better) as she said with her beguiling British accent, "It's not so much *me*. This one's (motioning to me) trouble! I always try to get out of it, but she has a live-in nanny, so I have no excuse!"

This time I did clock her!

Kidding!

I must admit, I actually liked this moniker. It was quite liberating for me to emerge from the drudgery of a mousy housewife persona, to a life and nickname (of *Trouble*) that connoted spunk, determination and vitality to me.

Our all-time favorite thing to do, however, was to get together at my place, cook dinner, perhaps invite a few other girlfriends, share some wine, chat about life, love, Botox and boob jobs. This way, our boys could be with us and play together while we giggled.

One of the new topics of conversation was all the interesting (that or mortifying—we weren't sure) talk of this hot mom/MILF concept. A married guy I knew told me I was one, and it was unnerving. I think it was around this time a song called "Stacey's Mom" was popular on the radio. It went something like "Stacey's mom has got it going on, I'm in love with Stacey's mom." It was a sign of the times. I even had friends, bartenders and others start to ask me about whether my older son's friends thought I was hot. *WTF! Really!?* That was a little creepy. Okay, it was a lot creepy. But the truth is, there was no shortage of cute, younger guys hitting on both Sheila and me. And trust me, we each indulged a little. But for the most part, anything meaningful with these MILFers, as we liked to call them, was unfathomable at least for me. I couldn't wrap my brain around the idea of being with a man who wasn't also my peer.

It Was A Super Jambalaya

*"We've **got** to go to Pat O'Brien's. It's a part of French Quarter history!"—Aaron Anderson*

The weeks went on after nabbing the Billboard Bash gig (as you may recall, my very first job in legitimate Hollywood-style television) and I learned of a vicious cycle that happens in the industry: procuring work, then working ungodly hours while at the same time relentlessly networking to procure more work for the future.

The only way I could survive the freelance nature of the entertainment industry was to do the best damn job of anyone EVER to prove my worth, and simultaneously lobby my ass off for future work opportunities during each production gig. I was still very new to this genre of entertainment (award-show talent management and producing) and a newbie in my position, which had a long line of both seasoned veterans and hopefuls, aggressively pursuing my job. I didn't *have* a long list of industry contacts or roster of relationships from being a staff member of previous shows. Even if I did, the whole business was very different after 9-11. Shows were disappearing, creating a mass of unemployed, talented and well-known production crew veterans. The competition, to say the least, was fierce. Established producers started taking production assistant jobs just to keep working. Plus, the entertainment business as a whole had changed.

I'd wager the cycle is pretty similar at the very top. You hear it all the time: some big-name director is dropped from next summer's huge film in favor of someone else, or one A-list actor is traded for another in a lead role. It happens all right. We just don't think much of it because we assume people at that level are set for life, never having to worry about it.

But think about it: Let's say I make $3 million a year on average with my mad directing skills, and say I only do three films a year. Then I sign on to do a huge film with a major studio. I'm now turning down other gigs as a result. If something goes south with that project, well, I'm out a HUGE chunk of money I was counting on to pay the mortgages on my three homes and my full-time staff of twenty, and at this point I've already told other projects no. Even if you add up all of my investments, if I can't come up with the cash I need to make my monthly bills, I, along with my staff, am going to be in just as much of a world of hurt—if not more—as the person relying on three-hundred-bucks-a-day gigs. So, the fact is, it's a continuous, vicious cycle, all so you can pay your bills and live the life of your dreams. It's cutthroat, I tell ya. CUT. THROAT.

That said, it's worth every ounce of worry, drop of sweat or lost hour of sleep, this fantastic field I landed in. I wouldn't have even *considered* trading it for a supposedly stable nine-to-five job. No way.

Although I remained the entertainment industry's networking maven (in between cocktails and fun times with Sheila, of course), attending events and talking ideas with other producers and industry professionals throughout the holidays, I also stayed in close proximity to my new friend, Aaron. I wasn't taking any chances. I had been a mere stand-in at the Billboard Bash, while Aaron's usual right-hand person was sick. I wanted to prove myself invaluable at every opportunity and make damn sure I was on his next show crew. I had no idea what his next project was, but I wanted to be on it.

Lucky for me (and Aaron of course), Aaron and I became good friends quickly. Our friendship was strictly platonic, and we kept each other in stitches most of the time with our rapid-fire jokes. I helped him move into a new apartment after a breakup and we set up an office down by the beach with his new business partners.

You want to know something truly hysterical and so typical of the entertainment industry? We spent a solid two friggin' months in meetings, brainstorming ideas for televised events and who to pitch them to, buying office supplies, designing and ordering business cards for this brand new production company and we never did one single, measurable thing with that company. There was no single event ever produced or pitched under its name! Typical Hollywood. When you hear people say, "Every person you meet in LA who says they're a producer is really a waiter, trying to break into the business," it's true. Everywhere you go, the person behind the register, the hostesses, waiters, bartenders, manicurists, Pilates instructors are all in LA looking for their lucky break. Many are actually working toward their goals, doing what they love, too.

The fact remains, while the few get their big break, the many wait tables, dog-sit and bartend to survive. They commiserate with acting class buddies and scheme the next big idea.

I can't tell you how much of my time I volunteered to help whip that office into shape, put together forms, write letters, discuss and investigate ideas for the exciting new company Aaron was putting together. But regardless of the outcome, it was exhilarating. You can't live or eat off that great feeling, but I highly recommend it. Pursuing your dreams is one of the most incredibly positive endeavors you can invest your time in. It fuels creativity and hope. So, I suppose you could say *that* is what the company "did." It fueled our creativity, and provided each of us a wonderful outlet during the holidays while everything was dead in Hollywood.

As the holidays came to a close and we entered the New Year, I began to make my intentions very well known to Aaron. Let's just say, I'm a pretty clear communicator. Remember my "cave-girl" tactics? Short of walking around everywhere flashing a blinding, blinking sign at him that read, "Hire me for the next show, Aaron!" I did and said anything I could to make it obvious. I needed work and my goal was to carve a niche in television, eventually producing on a show. It worked. As soon as Aaron came to his senses, he caved.

In January of 2002, Aaron brought me on board as part of his crew for the Super Bowl in New Orleans. We were hired by Tenth Planet Productions to handle talent logistics for the "Super Bowl Bash," the televised kick-off show for the Super Bowl's weekend of festivities. The show would air on CBS and involve musical performances by big stars and appearances by former football stars.

NFL players and their families were invited to the event, which would take place at the New Orleans Arena across from the Super Dome. I was thrilled to be part of the production team. I remember my first visit with Aaron to Tenth Planet Productions' offices, to discuss logistics. We learned there that the budget was extremely tight due to the extra security measures the NFL would have to take after 9-11. The league enlisted the aid of the United States Secret Service to handle security for every NFL-sponsored event. Back then, this actually meant something; now… maybe not so much. But security was no small task and quite costly. This budget constraint was the first of many similar cut-backs as a result of 9-11 we would experience in the coming months.

I realize it's difficult for anyone who wasn't at least 15 years old during the attacks on the twin towers at the World Trade Center, the Pentagon and the plane that crashed in Pennsylvania to realize or truly *feel* why 9-11 was such a big deal, or how it really made such a big impact. We humans are so freakin' desensitized now. We've watched the hanging of Saddam Hussein on live television; we heard in detail of the Navy Seal attacks that killed Osama Bin Laden, we've seen American journalists beheaded on YouTube, and we've been keenly aware of our nation's involvement in non-stop wars and entanglements in the Middle East since that time. Sadly, our tightened security and all that implies has become everyday happenstance.

Most people who were born during or after that period see the security measures taken at airports now as commonplace. It's all they know. We Americans who were adults, or lived and traveled at all before 9-11, viewed the attacks as the raping and pillaging of our freedom and our safety. We were slapped in the face with how naked and vulnerable we could be.

This frantic, nervous behavior that would elicit the NFL's hiring of the Secret Service for security was unprecedented, but it was also seen as necessary. Until then, Alist celebrities were turning down a free trip to the Super Bowl, even almost five months after the terrorist attacks, because they were afraid to travel and be a part of such a "high threat level" event.

This mentality, and the subsequent budget cuts, explains why the normal talent logistics crew of at *least* oh, maybe *eight* for a show of this magnitude would be cut to three. We knew we would have our work cut out for us, but I had no idea what was in store. If I think about it for too long, I can still feel the crushing pressure we felt during the first weeks of production on the show. As exciting as everything was for me, I was in W-A-Y over my head trying to handle the work of four different people.

I was initially responsible for all of the travel, hotel arrangements, and rider collection—the stipulations that artists would tack onto their performance agreements. They included audio and video equipment needs, but also items to be included in dressing rooms, on stage, and at their hotel. I'd heard of some outrageous requests, such as providing only the green Peanut M&Ms in the dressing room, but I hadn't experienced it until now. On this show, fresh white towels and bottled waters were required to be replaced stage right between every single song of No Doubt's set. But hey, that's entertainment!

I also handled ground transportation and Secret Service data and record collection for all of the talent on the show *and* their guests. At one point I think I counted up to 45 people in the *No Doubt* posse alone. Our show roster rounded out nicely with Sheryl Crow, Sting, Ja Rule, Ashanti and Martina McBride.

The Secret Service required all of these stars—some of them coming mid-tour from other parts of the world—to find a way to fax copies of their passports and details about themselves before they were approved for the show. Every single person on the show was required to undergo a background check. It was insane!

I remember getting a phone call from Sheryl Crow or No Doubt's road manager, who was in a little town somewhere in Europe with the band and he was a little perplexed as to how to make this happen.

And that wasn't the half of it. Most shows have one person doing the travel arrangements, another doing hotels and yet another managing ground transportation. I was responsible for all of this, as well as this little Secret Service security project and artist riders. Truly impossible for one person.

It wasn't long after we'd established the on-site production office at the New Orleans Arena when Aaron and I were summoned in to a meeting with some guy who worked with the NFL. All I remember was how freaking young he was, and STUFFY. And snippy. And in love with his power. The fact that this young punk was able to call Aaron and me into his office could have miffed anyone to begin with, but I'm all about success, so I went in with an open mind. Then he reamed us, which *really* upset me. That sucked beyond any tolerable sucking.

He asked me to print out and bring my hotel and ground transportation grid, which I did. Now, you must know that I'd never done this before. I was a dynamo in my own right and could make just about anything happen. But my wealth of experience making grids for gigantic Secret Service events added up to well…hmmm…let's see… ZILCH. The sum total of my relatable experience had been the nightly news in Albuquerque, New Mexico and the Billboard Bash (which was an incredibly *small* show, comparatively). So Mr. Punk NFL dude brought us to his little office and sat behind his big desk. He was almost too short to see over it as he picked my grid apart, questioned me about it and proceeded to tear us a new one. Aaron defended me (and himself), because he *knew* I was overextended and it was extremely unfair for them to put all of the responsibility on me, or any one person.

The next day, Tenth Planet Productions and the NFL paid to fly in three of Aaron's New York team to help us. Funny. It took the threat of our crew of three bursting into flames before they somehow miraculously eked out the money for more staff. But the damage was done. My confidence and pride were seriously bruised and I was sure Aaron was second-guessing his decision to bring me on. I couldn't handle that. But I'd be dammed if some little twerp with too much power would thwart my new career efforts! Screw him. Maybe getting the staff we needed was worth a little reaming, but I still wanted to roll up my three-foot-long Excel spreadsheet and shove it down his chubby little throat. Instead, I avoided him like the plague the rest of the production and went on about my business.

The two days leading up to the show were crazy. The New Orleans Arena was electric with excitement as the stage, lighting, sound and production crews readied for the show. Sting, Sheryl Crow, Gwen Stefani and company and the rest of the talent began to arrive and we greeted them, credentialed everyone, got them nestled into their dressing rooms, showed them the green room and made sure they were aware of their rehearsal and sound-check times. It truly was exciting! Everyone was pumped to be in New Orleans for a huge world-renowned event. We all had the events of September 11th on our minds and made it our mission to shine in spite of it all. There was a great feeling of pride.

Of course, we were all proud to be producing such magnificent music television, but more than that, it was the pride that we as a country had managed to pull ourselves up by our bootstraps and make this event happen, as expected, regardless of what any shithead terrorists might do or what scare tactics they might use. That we were about to parade in front of the entire world, including the countries who'd attacked us, the pinnacle of Western culture, the Super Bowl, and televise it live for the whole world to see, thrilled us beyond expression.

As the talent continued to arrive, Aaron or other members of the team greeted them while I took care of details for those still traveling. Our motley crew scurried around frantically making the green room, dressing rooms, stage and every other aspect involving talent perfect and ready to go. At one point on that first day of talent arrivals, I was walking from the production office into the hallway toward the dressing rooms and green room, and saw Aaron talking with a distinguished-looking man. At first I thought it was Sting, but Aaron motioned for me to come toward them and said, "Lisa, this is Billy Francis, Sting's road manager."

"Hi!" I said. *Wonder if he is related to Sting*, I thought.

"Hello, Lees-ur." he said in his sexy, British drawl, "Sting has sliced his wristband up a bit, and the Secret Service is frantic. Would you be able to replace his credential?"

Well, DUH. Hello? Am I a red-blooded female? Yes, sir! Right away, sir! Are you kidding me? I really didn't think I could contain the excitement I was feeling over how freaking COOL my job was, but I managed to say, "Absolutely! Come with me." I led the über-sexy Mr. Francis to my desk in the production office, where I kept the credentials (as well as the talent's Super Bowl tickets) under lock and key.

As I handed him the wristband, he said, "Oh no, I think you should do it."

Me? On Sting's wrist? Okay, FINE. Nag, nag, nag.

We headed toward the green room together. When we walked in I had my first look at the finished green room décor, something other members of the crew had worked hard on all day. It was fantastic. I'd not seen it since the first day, having been tied to my desk buried in travel arrangements. It was filled with really cool, white, contemporary leather furniture, two cocktail bars, a buffet of wonderful foods and snacks and food servers meandering about. The walls were covered with gigantic plasma screens. Sting's band, crew, other musicians on the show and a plethora of producers, writers, press and more were packed in there.

Billy walked me straight up to Sting and he turned to me and looked straight into my eyes. Billy said, "This is Lisa Jey, and she's got your new wristband."

"Oh! Hello!" Sting said pleasantly, and in his fabulous accent. "Thank you so much!" Photographers were snapping photos and I was the center of attention (yep, ME). I tried to hand him the scissors to cut the remaining wristband off, and he said, "I think you'd better do it."

"Okay." I said, and snipped it.

"Thank you!"

I know it was just a wristband, for goddsakes, but it was a banner-amazing moment for me. And, come to think of it, I think he liked me. I mean, I think he was really, totally and completely attracted to me. Uh-huh. No. I'm sure of it. I'm sure Sting still remembers and thinks about me to this day.

Let's go with that.

The next day was the day of show. As I was patrolling the talent dressing rooms (I would pop in to be sure everything was rider-compliant or there were no last-minute requests), I ran into Tracy Pearlman, who was running the event for the NFL. She was with and introduced me to her boss, the big kahuna of the NFL at the time, Commissioner Tagliabue. He was a tall, friendly man. He shook my hand and asked. "Lisa, I'd really like to have each of the artists autograph a football! Do you think they would be amenable to that?"

I laugh now at my ballsy answer, because really, who was I to say no, or make the Commissioner wait? He could have asked them to sing him a private personal song, if he wanted, I'm sure, and they would have happily obliged! But I replied without feeling or registering a single ounce of fear "Oh yes, I'm sure it would be okay, Commissioner! But let me run it by each of them and give them a heads up first. I'm sure they'd be happy to do it! Will you be close by so I can let you know?" He was very nice, and said that yes, of course that was fine.

When he and Tracy walked away, he probably clenched his jaw and said something like, "Who the hell does she think she is?" But I went right to work on it.

Everyone was totally cool about autographing the commissioner's football. There were a few priceless memories from that little project, as well. Gwen and the gang from No Doubt were totally cool, Martina McBride was super sweet. Ashanti hadn't arrived yet. In fact, I was surprised that Ja Rule and his gang were on site at all. On the day they were supposed to arrive in New Orleans, I received a frantic call from the driver who was meeting them at the airport. He felt sure he'd simply missed them, or perhaps they'd hailed cabs, but he could not find them.

I contacted managers, publicists and anyone I could think of to find out what had happened. After an hour or so, and much to my dismay, I received a call back informing me the band had missed their flight in Los Angeles. Not only was this stressful, there was no real solution. We'd booked the last remaining flight for them. Seats to New Orleans from Los Angeles were all sold out.

Their disheveled and very frustrated manager told me what he could: that the guys assured him they would arrive in time for everything. I sounded the alarm to the production crew, and Plan B was loosely constructed, should Ja, Incorporated *not* make it to New Orleans for the show.

Around 1:00 PM on the day of the show, sure enough, Ja Rule and his crew rolled into the New Orleans Arena. Apparently, stardom pays in spades, or private jets (which they'd flown in on). They promptly slipped in virtually undetected and took over their dressing room, crashing on every piece of furniture and throw rug in the place.

After getting a sweet "A-Okay" from Gwen Stefani about the autographed football, I knocked on Ja Rule's door, which was right next to hers. I'd barely seen the group file into the arena and I certainly hadn't met them. I had no idea what this guy looked like. I only knew the song he and Ashanti were singing in the show, "Always on Time." It was one of my favorites.

I waited for a response of some kind, but nothing. I knocked again. Nothing. Finally, I timidly grabbed the handle and started to turn it. As I pushed, the door opened, sounding like a suction cup, and smoke billowed into the hall. And it wasn't just any smoke, no. It was weed. A BUTT load of weed was being smoked in that room. The smoke alone almost made me instantly high. I coughed as I proceeded through the foggy layer, waving my hand so I could see, and asked a thug on the sofa, "Is 'Ja' in here?"

"Ja's" real name was Jeffrey, but I had no idea whether he answered to that. I'm sure it was a pretty funny picture to his friend: me in my little blondeness, inquiring for "Ja."

The guy on the couch opened his slitted eyes slightly and half shrugged, half-nodded.

I don't have time for this, I thought. I said, "Listen, Commissioner Tagliabue wants him to autograph a football, and he's on his way here, just so you know." I probably wagged my finger at the kid. I added, out of my innate sense of responsibility, and because I am a mother at heart, "This is an athletic facility, and there isn't supposed to be *any* smoking, let alone *this*." I laughed as I motioned around the room at the smoke, you know, to make him think I was as cool as possible after my little finger-wag.

"Okay," he said in his cool, chill, super-relaxed tone, "We'll find him and take care of it."

I wasn't trying to flatten him with my reprimand. I just knew I had to at least *say* it, in case it came up and I was asked. That was it. I had to trust the guy to "take care of it," because I still had other artists to talk to.

Next I went to my boyfriend, Sting's dressing room. I was sure I wouldn't see him. It would probably be one of his reps, or something. But I was excited about the possibility of seeing him again, anyway. I checked myself in the hallway mirror, before going in. I half-hoped it would be Billy. He was so nice-looking for a guy who was actually more age-appropriate for me than anyone else I'd met on these shows. Most production crew guys were twenty-something, if that.

Sting's dressing room was quite tranquil, with low lighting and tapestries on the walls. His manager greeted me at the door and I asked about the autograph. She called Sting over and he was just as engaging as before. He said, "I'll do it on *one* condition."

I smiled. *That I give you a kiss?* "What?" I said.

"If he'll give me a Super Bowl banner to take home. One of my kids collects them and they would be so excited to get one."

"I'll find out, but I'm sure it's not a problem."

He smiled, and half-jokingly said, "But only if he'll do that for me."

I walked out of his room, and apparently he was following me (of *course*). In the hallway was Sheryl Crow, who greeted him with a hug and said she was super excited to get to perform with him. It was funny. This all happened in a matter of a few seconds, and there was a staff photographer there to take photos. *What the hell? Are they inside the walls here?*

Sting is known for being in excellent physical shape, and Sheryl was flexing her biceps next to him for the camera. (Women celebrities and biceps... I tell ya). It was a fun moment. When Sting headed back to his dressing room, I asked Sheryl about the autograph and she said yes, of course she would, there was no problem. As I turned to walk away, I noticed Tracey Pearlman coming out of Martina McBride's dressing room with the commissioner, who was carrying a football and markers. *Huh.* I thought, *I guess they decided not to wait for me!* I'd already given everyone a heads up at this point, so it didn't bother me in the least. I walked up to them and said enthusiastically, "Oh! I was just going to come and find you both! Everyone said they would be happy to do it, but Sting asked if he could get a Super Bowl banner in return to bring home to his kids."

The commissioner and Tracey were hard to read. They seemed fine, but glanced at each other as if they were a bit surprised. Tagliabue smiled as he said, "I'm sure we can figure something out."

As the show was getting ready to roll, the frantic calls on the headsets gained momentum. I took a second to call Graden, who was at home with the nanny, and asked him to tune in to the show. I told him lots of famous people would be on the show and that I was working with them all. He was so freaking cute and recited back to me and then to his nanny as to which channel they should tune to. I hung up and breathed in. I hoped he was okay. I missed him so much.

I ran into Mr. Punk-Kid from the NFL at the end of the show. We had wheeled the bar from the green room into the production office, where we had all gathered to celebrate. Things had gone off without a hitch and the show looked fantastic. When he realized that Sting and his manager, as well as Sheryl Crow and Gwen Stefani, had taken a shining to me, as did all of the talent; when he saw that everything else went so well, despite his paranoia and his reaming us, suddenly Mr. Punk was friendly, even a bit flirtatious.

I had none of it. I didn't care who this kid was or whom he worked for. I would not be talked down to, or held responsible for their budget (or height) deficits. I wasn't vengeful, but it sure felt good to be able to snub him!

It sometimes takes me a while to catch on to what's really going on, but I eventually realized our staffing cutbacks weren't because the Secret Service was costing the NFL so much freaking money. It was because the NFL and television network greed-mongers didn't want to cut back on their own pay or profits. They wanted to keep the same amount of money (or more) as they'd grown accustomed to making, and squeeze the cutbacks out of the little people working on the show. *Stupid* NFL. *Big, stupid dumb* television networks. But I digress, again.

After the show, as the crew was wrapping up in the office (we weren't actually *done* in New Orleans, no), I started for my desk. Some of us were staying through to Fat Tuesday to help with Talent Logistics for MTV's Mardi Gras. Yes, for various reasons, the Super Bowl had been delayed and was taking place *during* Mardi Gras week. It was mayhem on top of sheer, unruly parties and flashing boobs. We were about to hit the French Quarter for one last night on the town with all of us together. I cringed.

During our first week in town—what seemed so long ago—we were all so excited we entered the French Quarter like school kids, me in particular. I'd never been to the city or any Mardi Gras celebration. We'd debated about where to go, but Aaron stated simply that Pat O'Brien's had to be our first stop, as it was the stuff of French Quarter legends. Well, that was it. I was done for from the start. The details are hazy, but here is a quick synopsis of *that* evening, as I recall or have been able to piece together from friend's stories:

1. I landed with the crew at Pat O'Brien's and promptly ordered the drink *du city*: the Hurricane. "Yummy! It tastes like Hawaiian Punch!"

2. Three (or four?) Hurricanes and some number of clubs later, I apparently made out with one of the crewmembers, a guy, thankfully (or maybe not thankfully, as he was not really my type).

But hey, they were lips on which I could land on, as opposed to, eh, falling down.

3. My neck was full of beads, and no, thank you very much, it was *not* from flashing my boobs! Remember, just a few short months before, I'd undergone a boob job and a scar/hernia repair on my belly! There would be no flashing of boobies. I quickly realized what a great negotiator I was even in my drunken state. I would catch all the young drunkies and say, "No, I can't flash you, but I will show you something really rad, because I just had,… duh duh duh duhhhhh…. *surgery!*" Every single guy "Wowed" in awe as I gave them a sneak peek at my beige medical tape across a wide incision on my belly. They promptly handed over their beads like they worshipped me. It was like taking candy from a baby.

4. At our final stop, a strip club, I could no longer manage my drunkenness. Apparently the group was not going to be allowed to enter because I could hardly stand up. I recall a tipsy Antonio turning to me, gripping my shoulders to keep me from falling over, and saying "Lisa! You have to act sober, okay? They won't let us in if you don't! Straighten up. Are you ready? I'm going to let go now, okay?" He would let go, and I would swoon over to the other side. Finally, Aaron took control of the situation and told Jim, one of the transportation guys who was not a drinker (and thus our designated driver) that he would have to take me back to the hotel. Jim was LIVID, to say the least. We started out toward the car, at first walking (me, staggering) along the quarter, and every few steps I would sit down to rest, on the curb, in the rain, with beer, urine and fill in the blank there in the curbside gutters. Jim kept telling me "Lisa! You don't want to sit in that shit!" *Literally.* Finally, he threw me over his shoulders, carried me to the car, threw me in and drove me back. He ended up putting me in a wheelchair and dumping me off at my room. The next morning, I experienced my first-ever debilitating hangover—which I *never* get. Truly. It was probably alcohol poisoning, as I could *not* move. Period. I wrote it

off to "cramps" the next day in the production office, and that is when the production guy I had made out with presented me with some Midol, as a super-sweet gesture. He had to email me to remind me about what had happened, and he was extremely nice about it, saying it was no big deal. *Whew!* I thought. *Because that was not going to happen!*

As I recalled our crew's first night in the French Quarter, I made a pact with myself that this time, though there would be some post-show fun, things would most definitely be different. My good-ole familiar vodka-tonics would do just fine. And water. Lots of water.

I got back to work prepping the Super Bowl tickets for the talent so we could get out of there. Looking back now, knowing what I know about the business, I should have stuffed two tickets for myself into my purse. No one would have cared. The NFL gave me charge over the tickets and filtered all non-show talent to request tickets from me. Nils Lofgren from Bruce Springsteen's E Street Band was one such artist who requested tickets and I happily obliged, which years later paid off in the form of seats and VIP lounge access to a Springsteen concert in Los Angeles.

While I was doling out tickets to performers and celebrities as I saw fit and the rest of the crew was packing up their things, I took a moment to check in at home. I turned my cell phone on to find a voicemail from my precious, adorable Graden.

"Mommy! You said you were on TV? What channel? I don't see you! Where are you?" It was so incredibly cute, my eyes welled up. I called him right away and tried to explain what I was doing.

He missed me and wanted to linger on the phone.

"I'll be back in a few days baby," I said. I knew this must have sounded like an eternity to him and my heart ached for him. I spent a few more minutes on the phone and reluctantly hung up.

As I was finishing the last ticket requests, Aaron asked for whatever tickets I had left over. Stupid *me* gave him all I had.

Once everyone was somewhat packed up at the office after our show, we commandeered one of the show limos to take us all into the French

Quarter. Our group consisted of Aaron, me, the audience/seat-filler guys (Rock, Mark and Bernie), Antonio and Jack and Jim from NYC. I was paying the piper to Jim, after his missing out on the strip club, and I spent the whole rest of the trip buying him Diet Cokes. We made our way into the quarter in our huge stretch limo.

This was the Friday night before Fat Tuesday in the French Quarter, and to say it was a party on the streets is an understatement. It was a squalid, filthy, exciting and enchanting bacchanalia of mesmerizing debauchery. Streamers flew through the air onto the mobbed streets. Balconies on every building contained a pile of zany, inebriated men and women, hanging over, flashing, begging for reciprocation and throwing beads into the crowd. It was a kaleidoscope for the senses.

We ran into various crews from our show—Sheryl Crow's crew and some of Sting's people. I managed my alcohol intake, so there would be no crewmember make-out sessions and there would be no hangover. But as a few of us meandered and danced our way from bar to bar, a flirtation with an adorable twenty-five year old audience facilitator, Mark began to brew. His family had a home in New Orleans and though he lived in NYC, he had a cute, distinctive accent. The attraction was mutual as we became friendly that night, dancing, drinking and having fun with all of our crew friends. When we headed back to the hotel, I was extremely glad for the day off that would follow. I knew I would need every bit of rest, as our work (and play) was not finished in New Orleans.

We all reconvened the next evening and hit some New Orleans hot spots. This was one of the very first times I ever encountered a ten-dollar cover charge for *women*. That was like thirty dollars these days. Maybe even fifty. I would never pay it. I mean, for guys, fine—but for chicks? And, well-dressed, pretty, fun chicks, at that? A few of the other female crew members and myself staged a coup and actually vetoed a couple of the hottest clubs, because they would not let us in for free. We were working on the SUPER BOWL events! Didn't they know who we were? I know. Ridiculous.

New Orleans is one of those few places in the country where the clubs are open all night. The fact many of my on-location gigs seemed to be in towns that never slept did not go unnoticed. But this is very dangerous. If you are out having fun, you can easily lose track of time. I stayed out all night and went to breakfast at dawn with Rock, Mark, Bernie and another female crewmember, Kristen. I only had eyes or attention for Mark. He was such a cutie. And regardless of what it was that was happening between him and me (fling, hookup, whatever), I wanted it. It was now Sunday, and dawn on the day of the big game and I still had to get to sleep. Oy.

My favorite team, the New England Patriots, was playing in the game and U2 was performing for half-time, yet I ended up having no way to see the game live. None of our crew had the time or ability to work on the halftime show, as busy as ours had been. But I hadn't even thought for a minute I would end up not going to the game. We went to the Billboard Music Awards, so why not the Super Bowl?

Funny. I slept a few hours that morning, then found out from Aaron I was invited to a party with some of the crew. Two other people and I were in a big empty house, basically. It didn't end up mattering much, I was so exhausted from the weekend, I actually fell asleep on the floor watching the game. But it was still a bit tragic.

Though I saw U2 perform their memorable halftime and I should have been all over the jubilation for the big game day, I went straight back to my room and was in bed early. Most of the crew was leaving the next day, except for Aaron and a few others who were staying behind with us for MTV's Mardi Gras, so things were finally winding down.

Though we had a blast working the Mardi Gras show, it was a minor gig compared to what we'd just finished. We basically helped MTV locate the celebrities when needed, who could be roaming around the facility they'd rented as the "backstage," (it consisted of three floors), and helped lead them to the MTV staff member in charge. That was about it. We were glorified talent wranglers for the show that had Carson Daly hosting, Brittney Spears, Gwen Stefani, Outkast and Blink 182, among others, performing. It took place outside, on a dreary and rainy day. We had to run the talent out under plastic garbage bags to ensure they stayed dry for as long as possible. It was fun, but nothing compared to our Super Bowl show.

Those of us who remained—Aaron, me, Mark, Rock and Bernie, Antonio and his girlfriend, and a few others—were invited to the premiere and after-party for Brittney Spears' movie, "Crossroads," that night. No, you probably have never heard of it, and if you have, it's a distant, foggy memory. More like a bad dream. The movie sucked and flopped. But we were all up for one last star-studded hurrah before returning home. I was glad too, because I really wanted to have some fun with Mark (insert wicked laugh).

After the party, not surprisingly, Mark and I went back to my room for a little romp. And why not? The guy was fit, young and drunk. We had some fun all right and it was Jerry Maguire style fun; vertical, up-against-the-wall, fun.

After about an hour of this, Mark felt the need to confess that when he drank, he was unable to, ahem, "finish" the job.

My reaction? "And, this is a problem?" Are you kidding? If the condoms are working, I can go on for hours, but the poor guy was a little sweaty and weak from over-exertion.

We laughed it off and chatted for a bit about how this was nothing serious, blah-blah-blah, "You're a nice guy, but," and "You're a super cool girl and really hot, but." So, we basically left it at that and it was fine by me. Thank you very much.

I boarded a plane the next afternoon. I was headed back home and back to the place I belonged, next to Graden at the dinner table. And oh, how it felt so right.

And The Grammy Goes To ...

"Come on Lisa Jey! Let's get out there and show them how to Salsa!" —Aaron Anderson

Waking up that first morning after returning from the Super Bowl/Mardi Gras was rough. I experienced more of that post-show depression I described after the Billboard Music Awards pre-show. This time, I recognized it as the lull that follows the fever pitch pace of production. I also knew I had to get busy booking my next show and fast. I no longer held a part time job for Gap Kids (the "real" job I'd taken when I first moved to town). I'd also let go of the event company gig (the one where I booked the wrap party for the Marilyn Manson DVD shoot). I was now a full-fledged freelancer in television production. I opened my eyes, grabbed the telephone and called Aaron. It was time for our morning "radio show," a recap of the previous night's (or week's) events.

Our "radio shows," as I mentioned, turned into some extremely funny exchanges between the two of us. On the occasions we couldn't make the call, we'd joke about missing our "shows": *They've started running our best-ofs, Lisa! We've got to get back before our listeners give up on us!*

If nothing else, it was great comic relief in the uncertain world of freelance work. Being the creativity addict that I am, I tried to talk Aaron into pitching our radio show to any one of his numerous connections so we could do our show for real, but I learned something new about Aaron in doing that: he was a restless individual, to put it simply. At that stage in his life, while still recovering from a harsh breakup, he was rethinking his entire life and career—thence the run at putting together his own production company.

The more I pressed him to pursue a real "radio show," the quicker I learned he was actually thinking of moving away from television production altogether. He'd gotten a bad taste of some drama in the industry and one day said to me "I'm subscribing to Mary J. Blige's mantra, Lisa. It's called, no more drama." In hindsight, it's probably good it wasn't an actual radio show. We would probably have been unemployed or sued pretty quickly.

I stepped slowly away from all manner of pressuring him and let the radio show rest. This was not the time to rock his boat. I wasn't able to see at the time how I could possibly continue to work in television if he ditched the production biz, so I let it alone and we continued to enjoy our phone calls for what they were.

After our usual fun banter, part of which included Aaron referring to my Ja Rule story as "opening the door to Hotel California to find a rapper," I learned that Aaron had two minor gigs coming up: a gratis (pro-bono) gig for his friend Sheila E. (formerly of Prince and the Revolution); and talent booking, logistics, and producing MTV's Rock the Vote show at the House of Blues. This thrilled me even more because the award winner would be my idols, The Dave Matthews Band.

Aaron hired me on both shows (big vote of confidence on the freebie job, I know). Both gigs were taking place during the Grammys, on which neither of us had jobs. I learned there were different crews doing the same jobs throughout the city. It made sense, as it would be impossible for us to work every show—many of them happened the same nights in different locations.

The first was the gratis job for Sheila E. and her business partner Lynn Mabry, who appeared in the recent award-winning documentary "20 Feet From Stardom" and who'd founded a charity called The Lil' Angel Bunny

Foundation, which was later renamed Elevate Hope. The charity brought therapy through the arts and music to underprivileged and abused children. It was holding their first annual fundraiser during Grammy week at Center Staging Studios in Burbank, which was also where many of the acts performing on Grammys rehearsed. We planned to capitalize on that fact and bring people to our show.

As soon as we met Sheila and Lynn in their office, I knew we had a really great group of people to work with. Once again, however, we were working on an event that was extremely short-staffed and on virtually NO budget. I helped book talent and celebrities, as well as write segments for the show. It was quite an undertaking, but I'll never forget it.

Sheryl Crow joined us once again and recognized me from the Super Bowl. Just like a best girlfriend she said, "I like your jeans! Those are cool! Where'd you get them?" Talking wardrobe with a superstar musician rocked (yes, pun intended).

Some other really great highlights: Stevie Wonder performed at the show and Sheila's family was the on-stage band for all the performances. This made for an incredible, long finale—Stevie is known for jamming the night away onstage, literally. You can't get him to stop.

Jimmy Smits was there to announce an award. Holly Robinson Peete and her hubby, NFL football star Rodney were on hand as announcers, and Snoop Dogg stopped by our stage the day before the show, inviting one of our crewmembers out to his car to get high. Forget about the fact that we desperately NEEDED that crewmember. We were running around like chickens without heads, but ahhhh, this was the life, working in production! As far as I was concerned, Snoop could come and steal our crewmember any time, at least that day. The story was worth every bit of anxiety.

*Sheryl Crow performing with Sheila E. and family
"An Evening With Angels" Fundraiser, 2002*

Some of the production crew and me with Stevie Wonder after the show, "An Evening with Angels" Fundraiser, 2002

The day after we wrapped Sheila's event, we dove head first into Rock the Vote at House of Blues (HOB) on the Sunset Strip. I hadn't yet worked an event at HOB, but learned every nook and cranny of that place pretty damn fast. I was excited about this show because the Dave Matthews band was the award recipient of the evening, and I was a *huge* fan. His lyrics were the stuff my dreams were made of and could make me coo and drool. Just sayin'.

The day of production, I remember walking through the venue, as the Goo Goo Dolls were loading in. As I walked across the main floor in front of the stage, a really cute guy with messy hair stopped what he was doing, stood up from behind some equipment crates, smiled at me and flirtatiously said "Hi!"

Oh geez, I thought. *A roadie is trying to hit on me.* I was used to them grinning sleazily at me and whispering under their breath to each other as I walked by during production. They would feel me up and down with their eyes. They did this to any girl not covered in warts.

Reluctantly and with as much disdain as possible, considering how cute he was, I said "Hi." I couldn't leave the guy hanging, but I had no interest. Even though he was super cute, I'd simply heard too many stories of roadies and their "sloppy seconds conquests" backstage with the girls the band didn't want. As I trotted up the stairs, walkie on my waistband weighing down my skinny jeans down with every step, I suddenly realized: *Oh my god! That wasn't a roadie! I think that was Johnny Rzeznik, lead singer of the Goo Goo Dolls!* How had it just *now* occurred to me? What? Was I new?! Why, yes. Yes, I was.

It's not that "lead singer guy" is more appealing than "roadie guy." Okay, he is. Just don't ask me why. My logic has been known to paralyze most with its incalculable and unfathomable reason. But basically it's kind of ludicrous because they're *all* looking for conquests backstage—not that there's anything wrong with that. So why would I give "lead singer guy" more thought than "roadie"? The fact that he, the superstar, noticed and stood upright to say hello when I walked by was a start— and that made me feel *good*. Not that I didn't (or anyone wouldn't) deserve it.

Plus, I won't lie. His life was way more exciting. I mean, let's face it: the roadies got the picked-over, clearance-bin perks in *every way* (obviously, those who are in committed relationships and not all about backstage lovin', excluded). The real perks of the business were reserved for the stars. If I was going to go "there" or anywhere, holding hands with a star was heaps more appealing. (I know. Sad). Plus, who's to say I didn't have some conquest notch of my own on my belt, when it came to lead singers? I didn't, but why not bash all stereotypes while we're at it? Plus *plus*, I *am so* the type to have that kind of notched belt, so there definitely *could* have been.

Nevertheless, I decided it was worth playing out to see if there was anything more. I casually sauntered back down the stairs in his direction and nonchalantly perused the buffet that was laid out next to the stage for the talent. I talk a big game about being ballsy, or super cool and the sexy kitten type, but it's all smoke and mirrors people. By the time I finally worked up the nerve to actually turn my head to *look* in his general *direction*, Johnny was gone. Boom. That fast, my dreams of being the famous *"Who's that sexy girl with _____ rock star?"* girl, who traveled around the country with her famous lead-singer conquest, went POOF, into thin air. As I kicked myself, I made a mental note: *Must be more aware of cute lead singers when they come your way!*

All was not lost, though. We had a long show ahead of us and were bound to run into each other. I'd be happy to slide a quick flirtation with him, next to my special-guest flirtation for the evening, Jorge, a Latin American record industry executive I'd met during Latin Grammys and stayed in contact with. I would have my hands full that evening, between Johnny Rzeznik and my soon-to-be-consummated relationship with the *real* "hot-n-steamy," Mr. Dave Matthews, (not to be confused with the one on *Grey's Anatomy*. Sorry Grey's fans!)

As the show progressed, however, it turned out that running into and flirting with Johnny Rzeznik (or any of my dream guys) was the least of my concerns. We were running around as crazy as usual. The event took place on the eve of Grammys, with all of our performers in rehearsals most of the day for their own Grammy performances or appearances at Staples Center area of downtown LA—not an easy commute to HOB in Hollywood. Los Angeles is difficult enough to navigate at the best of times, but our artists were coming to us during rush hour traffic. Add to that the thousands of extra people on the streets who were in town for Grammys, and the fact that our venue was on the Sunset Strip—well, let's just say our show ran extremely late, and it was going on television "live to tape." This meant it was live on the east coast, and would air on the west coast later.

As a result, we were extremely pressured to get the artists there, dressed and ready to go on stage as quickly as humanly possible. Once we started to notice how difficult it was for people to get to us on time, we started telling artists to arrive an hour earlier than we needed them for their sound check.

This worked until the Dave Matthews band actually followed our advice and ended up sitting for over two hours backstage while we awaited Nelly Furtado, members of Destiny's Child and other honorees. It got so bad, Dave and his guys started mumbling and threatening to leave. They were the night's main honorees. We couldn't have that.

The traffic issues and problems getting our talent to the venue on time were inching us close to failure. If one more thing went wrong on this show, there would be hell to pay. Under this pressure, we ran around trying to look like we were accomplishing things, when Aaron received a frantic call on the headset. Nelly Furtado's people still hadn't signed her appearance agreement. She'd been a last-minute addition to the Grammy performances and was stuck at her eleventh-hour rehearsal, and hadn't arrived at the venue, even though she was scheduled to go on momentarily.

The place was packed with guests and industry professionals at this point. The HOB decided to offer full dinner menu service, so there were guests dining upstairs, others in the bar and still more all over the place. Our task? Find Nelly Furtado's attorney, even though no one knew for sure what he looked like, and get him to sign the agreement in time for her arrival, so we could get her on stage to perform immediately.

Aaron put me on the job. I had to find the Executive Producer of Rock the Vote, Linda Field, and get further instructions. Linda was sitting in the sound booth with none other than Antonio, who was directing this show. As she handed me the artist appearance agreement, she said "We need this right away, Lisa!"

When I asked what the lawyer looked like, she had no idea, but she offered, "Look for an attorney-looking guy in a suit." I looked around. The place was covered in suits.

I got on the headset and asked the MTV staff for help. One of them met me and pointed out who she thought may be the guy. He was sitting at a table upstairs, eating dinner with someone. When I learned he was Nelly's attorney, I handed him the agreement and said, "Nelly can't perform unless it's signed." He took his time to look it over, while I heard over my headset that the Dave Matthews Band was calling their car to leave. Aaron knew I was on the Nelly Furtado problem, so he left me out of it, but I could hear all the yelling and crying.

Hurry up! I thought, as Nelly's attorney looked the agreement up and down. He had a sort of sleazy grin on his face, as he looked at me and said, "I can't sign it like this." *Are you kidding me?*

It's a good thing I've worked just about every job known to woman, because almost any other production crewmember—especially one who was new as me—could have easily cowered, said "Okay," and walked away crying. I quickly retorted, "You're an attorney, feel free to mark it up so it's acceptable."

He was a little surprised, to say the least, as he took the document back and sneered, "Okay, but you're going to have to wait. And don't stand here waiting. I'll come find *you*."

"Fine," I said, and shrugged as I walked off. I immediately reported it to Linda on the headset.

Linda was mad as hell. "Let him know she won't go live, if we don't get that back!" she yelled. So, of course I had to go back to the table and deliver that lovely news. *Good!* I thought, *Serves the guy right.*

As soon as I had a spare moment, I let Aaron know I was waiting on Nelly Furtado's attorney.

"Lisa, the Dave Matthews band is not happy and about to leave," he said. "We can't let that happen. Can you do something?"

"What? Like, buy them a round of drinks?" I answered.

"I don't know Lisa, I've got my own issues with the Goo (Goo Goo Dolls) in their dressing room. Can you just handle it? Get the house person on the headset and work something out."

Hang out with Johnny while I handle my other love interest. Fine.

The "house person" was the event person who worked for the House of Blues. I got her on the headset and decided that rather than simply offer to buy them drinks, we would give them their own personal cocktail waitress, to bring them "things and stuff." In my world, that means whatever they wanted from the House of Blues.

I didn't have time to gush or be nervous. I walked up to the band's "dressing" room—more of a meeting room, with tables and chairs—imaging them raging about show delays, managers and agents running around with their hair on fire, but no. It was just the band and perhaps a few friends, talking quietly. I walked into a room that was super-mellow.

It was like an album cover: my future love-slave (I can dream) Dave was sitting in the background with his band members in the foreground. I walked right up and said, "Hey guys, I'm sorry about all of the delays, but we want to try and make you all as comfortable as possible, while we deal with the horrors of everyone arriving in this traffic. How about if I bring a cocktail waitress up here to take care of you guys? Would that be okay?"

The guys started to nod at me and at each other and a few of them said things like, "Yeah, that'd be good." The house gal immediately called a waitress in. This was the obvious right solution, as the band was chuckling now. We'd at least broken the sound barrier.

"House" gal said she would take it from there, so I said goodbye to the band. And THAT, my friends was the extent of my hot-n-steamy affair with Dave Matthews.

I stepped out into the hall and back into fire drill mode. Nelly Furtado had arrived and apparently a member of her staff got a little pushy with a female crewmember. Linda Field was on the headset, yelling out into space, "Lisa, any update on Nelly's release?" *Good thing I just tuned in,* I thought.

"Not yet, Linda. I'll go get it from him."

"Yeah. Tell him she won't go live if Nelly doesn't get on the stage and I don't get that release NOW."

Just as I was racing to find Mr. Sleaze attorney, there he was. It's like these guys were in the walls right next to the photographers! He just stepped out of a corridor, as if to block my passage, agreement in hand. It was marked all over the place in red, barely legible, but I took it. Just for grins I said, "Oh, and Linda Field wanted me to let you know Nelly won't be going live if she isn't out there right now and because of the delays on this, she may not go live at all."

I turned the volume back up on the headset just in time to hear "Lisa: Go for Aaron."

"Go for Lisa."

"Lisa, can you go down to Nelly Furtado's dressing room and see what's going on? Be careful though, a member of her posse is getting a little feisty." He chuckled. *There's my fun friend!* I thought.

I went downstairs to where they were keeping Nelly, which had two entrances. The stars were aligned in my favor in that moment, because I arrived at one door just as another of our crewmembers was "engaging" with Nelly's watchdog in the other doorway. I looked directly at Nelly and said, "They need you onstage now. Like five minutes ago."

Nelly was adjusting her belt in the mirror and nonchalantly turned a deadpan, disinterested look toward me. She turned back to the mirror and continued to adjust her belt a micro-millimeter without even saying so much as an "okay." Her staff member turned toward me.

"Tell her to get out there now, or she won't go on," I said.

"She can't go out until she's ready."

I looked at Nelly, who was not responding at all, bringing all the DIVA she could muster. I looked back at her gatekeeper.

With the stone-cold gaze I've become known for (used rarely, but yes, it's a hallmark) I said in the coldest, most evil, threatening tone I could whip out, "She's ready enough for us. Just know she will **not** go on. And *if* she does, it probably won't be live if she isn't out there NOW." I turned on my heel and walked off. *Big, stupid, dumb diva artist. She probably didn't even know what "go live" meant.*

What it meant was her performance on stage would not be part of the live broadcast shown on the east coast and would only make the taped version for the west coast, if time permitted editing it in. More than likely she wouldn't make it to the broadcast at all, and at best, the local audience at the House of Blues would be the only people who would get to see her performance.

I was so glad to hear that news about Nelly's performance possibly not being broadcast. I'd experienced my first divalicious moment, and there was nothing "licious" about it. The whole diva thing, and the popular belief that it was cool and empowering to be a diva back then, was a LIE. Nelly Furtado was rude and did absolutely nothing while a member of her staff physically accosted a woman who was simply doing her job, a job working on a show that was only going to further promote *her. Good for MTV.*

I cared too much then, and you would think Nelly and her management cared then too, but really, think about it: where is she now? She was one of the hottest things in 2002, and now, she struggles to make a name for herself just like every other momentary pop star. I blame mismanagement and her arrogance. You didn't see Tom Cruise acting arrogant. But, all I can say is meh. I don't care so much anymore. I simply have no tolerance for arrogance at any level. And even as I write this, who knows? She could be making deals to turn things around and become a household name again. For all I know, she's living the high life right now, raking in millions as one of the smartest divas ever. If so, let's hope she's grown up.

It was funny. I'd been so busy with everything, I'd barely had time to say hello to my special guest of the evening, Jorge, a Latin America executive for Sony Discos (Sony Records). I'd managed to get him into the event, even though it made Aaron question his need to be there. He was married, but super cute. The last I saw of him that evening was in the dining room where I'd confronted Nelly's attorney.

It happened that when Nelly Furtado finally performed on stage, Jorge asked, "Who is that girl?" I found it hard to fathom that someone in the music business could be so ensconced in his or her own music genre that they had no idea of what was going on in other realms. He knew every artist that graced Latin American radio, but although Nelly Furtado spoke Portuguese and many of her recorded songs included lyrics in the language, THE MAIN MAN at Sony Discos didn't know who she was. Fancy that.

The fact that Jorge was "interested" in Nelly only made me more upset about the diva. Not that it mattered. He was married anyway. He would never be anything to me for real, but I was miffed because he was *my* fantasy flirtation.

I was fuming as I left the HOB parking lot for home. I turned on the radio and sang along to none other than the Dave Matthews Band.

At home, I snuck into Graden's room and kissed his little forehead. He was sweaty and snuggling his new puppy (a gift from his dad, of course), Puggy, beneath a pile of his favorite stuffed animals. *My little cutie,* I sniffed. How I missed tucking him into bed at night. But I could be there in the mornings, and made sure I was.

The next morning, I made pancakes for Graden and me, packed up an extra-special lunch for him as he played with his little Puggy, and walked him to school. These were the best moments for me. We'd paid extra money for training for Puggy and we practiced everything we'd learned on these morning walks to school.

Back at home, I received a call from Aaron. During our "radio show," he reminded me we were invited to a post-Grammy party at the Conga Room, a club owned partly by Sheila E. and Jimmy Smits. I in turn, reminded Aaron that the following week he promised to be my "date" at an engagement party for my friend Adrienne. I was to be a bridesmaid and I didn't know many of the other gals in the bridal party. Bringing my comic relief to the party sounded awesome. Aaron assured me he was in and we made arrangements to meet at the post-Grammy shindig.

At the Conga Room that night, I found Aaron and his friends from the "production company," Kevin, Alan and the limo driver Matt, waiting in the standing-room-only area. The place was packed, and then we saw Lynn Mabry and Sheila, who were greeting people as they saw them. They always have been incredibly sweet and kind. Lynn said to grab a table if there was one, and not to be shy about it. We found a fantastic table just to the left of the bandstand, right above the dance floor.

It was incredible. Grammy nominee Tito Nieves performed with the full band As we watched the people salsa on the dance floor, I felt like I'd been transported to another country, or to the set of *West Side Story*. The music was intoxicating and the band was better than the best.

Aaron grabbed my hand and said, "Come on Lisa! Let's show 'em how to salsa!"

"Okay!" I said. I had no idea how to salsa, but I could fake it. We had so much fun, dancing and sweating it out after such a crazy month.

I went home that night, with an entire week of recuperation and catch up ahead of me. Aaron had informed me of another pro bono job that was coming up, the Mint Jubilee—the same event I'd been to, *had it been a year??* since I'd met him, Antonio, Brian and so many others? I wasn't about to miss that one, but I was glad to have a week to put some things in order and spend more time with my little guy.

Somewhere in there, my bestie Sheila and I made an appearance at a popular nightclub called Barfly on the Sunset strip. It was a school night, but we didn't care, and Sheila waited until we were there to inform me that her boyfriend (with whom she'd been fighting) might be there with his friends. He was, there and by some mysterious coincidence, she ran into him. Then she left with him. Figured.

For my part, I met a group of cute guys who were all part of a bachelor party. One in particular was very interested in me and kept trying to buy me drinks. He looked so much like Justin Timberlake, it was stunning. The groom looked young and timid. I asked how old he was and was shocked to hear twenty-one—shocked and a little sad that a guy so young was getting married. I couldn't help but think he was in for a huge life trial when the marriage eventually unraveled. It was an unfair assessment, but statistics supported my outlook more than his, and hey, my divorce had just recently become final (on Valentine's Day no less).

After a couple of cocktails, my little Justin Timberlake said, "Hey my friends have a suite next door at the Mondrian hotel, and they've got a full bar and stuff. Do you want to come have a drink?"

HELL no.... But he was very persistent. After I hemmed, hawed and tried to wiggle out of it because it just wasn't *right*, JT assured me there was a whole party going on in the suite. He motioned for the bouncer of the bar to come over, who knew him and vouched for him. He also called his friend's cell and asked him to talk to me. There *was* a very loud party underway and I could hear several girls laughing and joking in the background, so we were off. The cutie patootie held my hand as we walked down the block to the Mondrian Hotel and to the bachelor party suite.

Uh-oh. What have I gotten myself into now?

I wasn't there very long, but he was a sweetie. He worked for a professional basketball team (perhaps you've heard of the Lakers?) doing stats, was ambitious and just altogether super cute. I know, I know. I apparently still can't get over his cuteness. We were just sitting there, hanging out visiting with his friends, when suddenly he kissed me. *Oh boy, this is good*, I thought, just as someone grabbed my camera and snapped a picture of us face-macking. I sat up and promptly left the party. I had no business making out with a twenty-one-year-old, or whatever age he was, let alone getting *photographed* in the process.

JT and I exchanged phone numbers and continued a kissing romance for some time —if you can call one additional kissing date, along with a few late night phone calls where he professed his undying love and infatuation with me, a romance. Ah, but young people are easily distracted (and apparently I was distracted by young people!) so that little romance simply faded into oblivion.

It's Raining Men

"Yeah. She's definitely got her groove on." he joked. "All that dirty dancin' shit. She looks like she's fucking the guy."—Rock (audience guy)

I'm not going to sugarcoat things for you here. If you didn't notice this from the previous chapter, there were men-a-plenty in my life at this point. You might say it was "Mantastic" (sorry). As I journeyed further down the road away from my divorce debacle and closer to rediscovering the "me" I'd lost in the marriage, guys seemed to come out of the woodwork in all shapes, ages, sizes and financial statuses. What paradigm shift in the universe happened that attracted so many men to me? I dunno.

I can *guess*. For starters, it probably didn't hurt that I was willing to go hard-core on my own ass and whip myself into shape. Also, I think men are especially attracted when a girl is busy just trying to make things happen and isn't so concerned with finding a man to rescue her.

But I actually believe it's more ethereal than that. I've seen time and again in my life, when I make bold, courageous moves in favor of my well-being or for ME, the response is a resounding attraction of people and things to me. Not to go all woo-woo or spacey on you here, but it's an age-old concept that's been said in many ways: "you reap what you sow," "you'll attract what you put out there," "what goes around comes around," or whatever other phrase we've heard and repeated since we could speak. When I treat "me" well, others come around and do so as well!

It seems when I take bigger risks, my returns in life experiences, opportunities, etc. tend to be even bigger. At this point it seemed to be raining men. My response? Get out the galoshes and start "singin' and dancin' in the rain."

Brit's career was taking some twists and turns, and aside from a lunch date or girls cooking night here and there, playtime with her was rare. That did *not* mean my propensity for fun or "trouble" quieted. I wasn't about to let her tight schedule stop me from enjoying life and exploring. Sheila and I, on the other hand, found all the more time to cultivate our friendship (with equal parts mischief), and it simply felt *right*. As I said, she felt like family to me. We could share all our fun, girly desires and stories and divulge our deepest secrets, worries and concerns as well. Friendships like that are not found easily, especially as one gets deeper into adulthood, when most friends are paired off or raising families. I think it's even *more* difficult to meet birds of a feather in a large metropolis like Los Angeles.

I've already attested to the fact Sheila and I laced our free weekends, even some "school" nights, with visits to Hollywood nightclubs, entertainment industry or music industry events and wrap parties for some of the shows I was working on. It wasn't all we did. We still cooked together and loved getting together with our boys. Our fantastic luck with our sons becoming friends and the willingness of my nanny, Muriel, to take on regular sleepovers didn't escape us, even after she told us that putting those two boys together was like adding gasoline to a fire. We took advantage of as many opportunities as possible (and feasible) to get out and play.

One such evening occurred while Marcus was visiting Graden and Joel with his new fiancé, Jewel (no, not the pop-star). By this time, things were amicable between Marcus and me. Hey, the fact that he was staying sober was a giant bonus, but that he desired the connection with the boys again meant a lot. I opened my home to him and Jewel while they visited and toured Hollywood, Beverly Hills and the beach. When they would return, arms full of shopping bags, Jewel gleefully displaying the new expensive clothes or shoes Marcus had purchased for her, I smiled and enthusiastically *oohed* and *aahhed* over her loot. I was happy for the goodies she'd received. I really was. But I also could remember clearly the days when Marcus showered me with more than I could or should have, even against my wishes and protests. Having experienced the heavy baggage stapled to those gifts, I couldn't help but think *Drink it in now baby, 'cause when he's confident he's got you, the thrill over the shopping sprees will be gone.* I truly felt bad for her, for that day, because at some point in the future that realization would strike her.

On this particular trip for Marcus and Jewel, I was working on a little show called the Soul Train Music Awards, produced by Don Cornelius Productions, which also produced the Lady of Soul Awards.

In order to put this evening into perspective, I have to rewind to how I got the gig in the first place. Aaron had nothing to do with my working on this show. No, this one came about through a very different kind of man, in an extreme and unique way. It reminded me of Hollywood folklore, which generally results in studio contracts for beautiful young starlets.

I didn't get a three-picture deal from this Hollywood-style happenstance, but here's what *did* go down: I was unassumingly basking in the beauty of a mani-pedi at my neighborhood nail spa on Westwood Boulevard, when in walked an African-American man with big brown eyes and a bright white smile. He looked right at me. We chatted a bit and he was extremely pleasant. I remember thinking how refreshing it was to be around someone who was so, well, *happy*. He didn't really say all that much to me, though I don't remember much of what we did speak about. One thing I'll never forget is what happened when my nails were done: I tried to pay my bill and was informed that Mr. Nice Guy, who'd already left, had paid my bill and left a note for me. The note read simply:

"You have a gorgeous smile.

Someone so pretty shouldn't have to pay to have her nails done."

He also left me his business card. I smiled and was a little embarrassed. Why was I embarrassed? Well, DUH – because I just knew the women in the nail spa had to be talking trash about me every single time I went in there—not because I am insecure, but because they could without my understanding them. Hell, I would! Ha ha! And suddenly, they were ALL eyeing me with silly-ass grins on their faces. Listen. Who doesn't think those women are talking to each other in front of you in their own language, giggling over how foolish they think you are, while they nod and smile at you? Trust me. They do it.

When the woman at the front desk informed me of the news, and I realized everyone in the salon was quiet and smiling at me, I thought *Are they happy, or mocking me?* I didn't know, but I got the hell out of there. I didn't care what *they* thought, but this was MY surprise.

It was actually one of the coolest things to ever happen to me, even taking into account working with celebrities and all the cool parties and limos. Men had tried to woo me in the past, but this was bold, unanticipated and a total surprise. "Wow." I smiled widely to myself, "I love LA."

Then I did what any decent girl would do, regardless of the fact that said Mr. Good Samaritan was a complete stranger and common sense would advise against it: I called to thank him.

His name was Kenny. He was very nice, and we struck up a phone friendship that carried on for a few weeks, before I invited him to come to my home with other friends for dinner. I cooked a fabulous feast, and Kenny arrived early with a gift of expensive perfume.

Uh oh, I thought. I wasn't *totally* surprised. I'm not an idiot. But I thought I'd have more time to make my intentions, or lack thereof, more obvious. Other men had attempted to buy my affections in the past, not just Marcus, but Kenny was non-threatening and low-key. He had a wonderful spirit. He was extremely sweet and kind, but I was simply not attracted to or romantically interested in him. I knew no other way but honesty. I was never one to fawn over someone or feign interest just to get the goodies, or to promote my career or status.

Kenny was a gem and a gentleman about it. He acted as though he knew my intentions were true and honest. When he learned I was working very diligently to branch out from Aaron and increase my work portfolio in television production, he offered to set up a meeting for me with Tony Cornelius, the son of Don Cornelius from the show Soul Train.

He had to educate me to get me to understand the gravity of such a meeting. He explained that the Lady of Soul Awards and the Soul Train Music Awards were extensions of the television show Soul Train, all of which were produced by Don and Tony Cornelius.

It was Kenny's connection, coupled with a little diligence on my part, that finally landed me a gig assisting the PR company for the show, Rogers and Cowan, in setting up the red carpet. The award show was taping while Marcus and Jewel visited. Because I had also struck up a friendship with Tony Cornelius, I was able to invite Jewel and Sheila to the show and after-party.

It always felt pretty awesome when friends and family from Albuquerque, New Mexico would come to town and I could provide a little behind-the-scenes action for them. We attended the after-party and nabbed a few gift bags. It was loads of fun.

My takeaway from events like this is just how *few* of the artists and celebrities actually attended the "official" after-parties. *We* were there, and not to knock our fabulousness in any way, but we were not stars. We watched as record label execs and their arm-candy wives or girlfriends (or boyfriends, HELLO) filed in, but I couldn't tell you a single star that we saw that evening at the after-party.

I'm sure Sheila and Jewel had more luck in the auditorium watching the show. I introduced Sheila and Jewel to Tony. Sheila and her beau were on a "break" and, well, how do I say this? Sheila needed a little Hip Hop in her step and Tony was right up her alley. I made it my mission to introduce them and set them up. The moment came, and it was like you could hear the world's biggest balloon deflating. The flatulent kind.

It was almost comical. No attraction. None. Zilch existed between the two whatsoever.

Tony later took me to lunch and said that I was probably more his type. This was new for me. I'd always been the friend who was passed over because guys were more into my girlfriends like Brit and others. And I was a bit perplexed too, because Sheila looked like Michelle Pfeiffer! Why *wouldn't* Tony be attracted? At this point I had to ask myself why the hell the guys I wasn't interested in were the most willing to pursue me. But I was just as honest with him as I was with his friend Kenny, and we remained friends. He continued to hire me for award shows after that point as well, proving what a class act he was, and I'm sure he still is.

Sheila, Jewel and I left the after-party and headed back to my place to pick up Marcus. He agreed to be our designated driver so we could go to whatever hot new Hollywood nightclub we could think of. We had a friend who was the head bouncer at one of the hottest nightclubs of the month. We were in.

This particular night, since Sheila and her man were on the outs, it wasn't long before we were getting our groove on with guys half our age on the dance floor. In our defense, "guys half our age" were the status quo at these nightclubs, and the only ones to ask us to dance. We liked to dance, so it was just part of the deal. Ninety percent of the guys were too young and the other ten percent were either taken or gay. As Britt told me, "In LA the rule is, 'They're gay unless proven otherwise.'" She was pretty accurate on that one. We sucked it up, enjoyed a cocktail or two and shook our booties.

While still sober, Sheila implored me to prohibit her from going home with a young guy, *or* taking one home. Her weakness for younger guys, who seemed to be undeterred by our age, had not escaped her. Not that she was promiscuous, but she anticipated the rebound feelings she might experience after a few cocktails and knew to forewarn me.

She cracked me up with her British accent. She so properly pleaded with me to be stern and "under no circumstances" should I allow it, "no matter what," even if she tried to change my mind.

I was definitely up to the task. If a hot guy started getting too close, I went all "grizzly" up in his face. I'd rapid-fire things at the poor kid like "You know I have a son that's almost your age?" "My girlfriend here is *my* age." That was bad, but hell, I had to use whatever would work. "She needs a man with a career, who can buy her nice things and spoil her." "Go find someone else to teach you sex tricks, buddy!"

I *think* Sheila appreciated it, but as the evening wore on, the bargaining began. She tried hard, but I wouldn't have any of it. Far be it from me to forego my responsibilities to a girlfriend.

I'm not quite sure how I won, but somehow we all left the nightclub together.

Ah, the memories of it all are recalled with a wry, but sweet, sarcastic sense of humor: me, Sheila, my ex-husband and his new fiancé clubbing in Hollywood together. I actually loved the irony and the fact that I was FREE and not at all tied to the man but could honestly enjoy a night out with him and his fiancé. Was it a little strange? Oh yeah. But it was classic.

A day or so after Marcus and Jewel returned to New Mexico, Aaron called with an invitation to accompany him and his new partners to Palm Springs. He wanted to make a fun night out of it, as one of our production friends, Rock, wanted to meet about bringing Fashion Week to Los Angeles. Yes, Rock did accomplish this. Well, someone did. But he had the idea long before any LA Fashion week actually ever happened. Aaron told me that if I came along, I could bring a friend, we would take the limo and be back before the night was through. It was a no-brainer, so Sheila and I jumped aboard our own personal "Palm Springs Express," with another fun, interesting crew.

I'm not quite sure what was going on at the bar we ended up at in Palm Springs, but Aaron knew the promoter and it was some sort of event with C-list celebrities attending. Sheila and I had no idea who the celebrities were. This actually happens quite a lot in Southern California. With the advent of reality TV and so many new networks, there are thousands of characters clamoring for their fifteen minutes of fame.

At that time, reality TV was made up primarily of The Real World and a few other shows, like Antique Road Show or some other permutations of the concept. I rarely took the time to watch the shows I *worked* on, much less other forms of reality television, which I found uninteresting (and still do). I've never quite understood the fascination with watching other people's everyday lives unfold on national television, even the extreme dramas that are caught on tape, which seem unbelievable. I really don't care that much but I suppose therein lies the allure: getting that peek into someone's life while something unspeakable happens to them.

As the medium progressed, however, it became less and less real and more scripted. Rumors spread about producers feeding scenarios to cast members, who would act out situations. We'd even heard of producers telling the cast to basically restate questions. So, the question may be, "Why do you think [cast member] is such a slut?" Then the person is forced to say "I think [cast member] is a slut, because_____."

I know one gal who was on a reality show and was dating a fellow cast member. When the relationship went awry off camera, the producers convinced them to break up again on camera, even going so far as to recreate a similar environment to the actual event for them. All this is done to attract an audience.

I suppose it was bound to happen in order for shows to constantly crank out strong ratings and get picked up for additional seasons. And the reality TV "stars" are all too willing to create fake drama for good ratings.

In any case, someone from one such reality show was being promoted that evening. Sheila, Aaron, Kevin and our friend Rock took the opportunity to imbibe and indulge.

It was clear pretty early on that Rock, though he was trying to play it cool, found Sheila attractive. As the afternoon and evening turned into night, and we'd gotten our drink on for some time, Sheila was out on the dance floor shakin' her business. Rock was checking her out and that's when he laid his little philosophy on me.

"Yeah. Sheila's definitely got her groove on." he joked. "All that dirty dancin' 'n' shit. She may as well fuck the guy right there." He continued, "Yep. She definitely wants to fuck him."

"No way! You are SO wrong." I insisted.

I spent the next twenty minutes on an impressive diatribe about women and their true need for affection: how they never want to have sex for the sake of sex. How that even if women *say* they do, they're not being honest with themselves, because women always get emotionally involved. I can look back now and know that I said this mainly because the sting was still burning from my fling with Antonio. I'd thought I was in more control and that our casual affair was manageable, but I'd wound up confused over it all.

I stressed all of this with matter-of-fact, "I'm an expert and you are not" dogma, of course. I convinced him that I was arguing the contrary because I was his *ally*. If I were correct, well, Sheila was still fair game for him. If not, we may as well part enemies (playful enemies, of course).

"Bet me," he said.

"What?"

"Come on! Put your money where your mouth is! Bet me! We'll ask her when she comes back," he bullied.

"I never bet for money." I waffled.

"Fine. We'll just bet a drink. If I'm right you're buyin'!" he said with a conquering grin.

"Awesome!" I sipped my cocktail through my straw, wiggled to the music and tried to look confident.

After a couple of songs, Sheila came back to the table. Within two seconds she threw me under the bus.

"Tell us, Sheila," Rock said, mocking me with every syllable, "When you were dancing with that guy, rubbing your body next to his, was it because you want a relationship or 'Need affection'?"

"What do you mean?" Ms. Demure asked.

"Lisa here thinks that women all do that shit because they want a relationship."

"Hell no!" she said, with an overly English-heavy-accent, "I just want to fuck him!"

As I passed around the round of drinks I purchased, I reflected on what had just gone down. I was a little baffled. What was different about Sheila that she could so quickly say she "just" wanted to fuck a guy? Sheila was the epitome of well-educated, well-traveled and cultured. She'd lived in France, Spain, and Japan and had learned a bit of each language. She was extremely kind, funny and smart. It was all so shocking and so new to me. Sure, I'd had my fair share of no-strings dalliances, even before this, but I chalked them up to my "finally free" shenanigans. Sheila was many years a single mom, and yet she held this belief, or so she said.

With much deep thought and self-exploration (for oh, about ten minutes), I conclude that "Yes, damn it. Women *should* be able to have senseless, unattached, unadulterated sex if they want to. They should be able to think of *guys* as MILFs (Men I'd Like to Fuck) and say it out loud, if they wanted to." If my gorgeous, well-adjusted girlfriend from England can do it, then what was the hangup with most women I'd ever known? What was *my* hangup? Why had everything I'd ever read or heard made it sound so bad, or at minimum, inauthentic if women wanted that rip-your-clothes-off, in-the-moment, non-committal sex that men have traditionally looked for? Was it just something we Americans were hung up on?

I didn't know, but I decided I would have no more of it. Determined to be the "continental girl" I'd always admired, I make a conscious decision to adhere to the philosophy that women can truly enjoy physical pleasure without attachments (given the right situation, of course).

Shortly after that, I (sort of) made it my mission to find me one of those sit-ee-ations.

How I Saved Aerosmith From Ms. Bitchy Bitch Bitch From Bitchville

kkhhh ... "Lisa! I need you to go find Jack Black and give him his credentials ... Over!" kkhhh—Aaron Anderson

You may recall, my first glimpse into entertainment television production happened when Britt and I traveled first-class to Louisville, KY, fresh off my hostile separation from Marcus. When my therapist suggested a change of pace, there was no way in hell she could know how much change I could bring into my life. Talk about stepping into a brand new world.

A year later, I had observed enough of Aaron's personal and professional life to know that the guy loved to have his posse with him at work and at play. Unfortunately, sometimes, when people thought they were being brought on for a paying gig, well, that didn't always happen. They were there, and they were put to work, but ... Aaron didn't always have enough in his budget, or proper authorization, to actually *pay* everyone. It was one of the drawbacks of doing business with him. If you didn't ask very clear and precise questions like, "Am I going to be an official staff member, Aaron, or is this another one of your 'I'll pay you out of my pay' deals?" well, chances are you were out of luck. It hadn't happened to me, thank God, but I was smart enough to know I wasn't immune. And as his right hand on many productions, I dealt with my share of angry people over these types of situations.

There was never a dull moment with Aaron, though. We'd only had a week off and were already in meetings for the next Mint Jubilee show, just ahead of the Kentucky Derby in May. While on our way to a Jubilee meeting, Aaron received a call and we were hired to work on MTV Icon. Icon was a little show that MTV did for about four years in the early 2000's where they honored a select icon of rock-n-roll. That year, the honoree was Aerosmith. It was going to be a big show, by MTV "little show" standards, and Aaron had a full staff.

This time there were some new players I'd never worked with, and from day one, the tensions were high. One in particular I'll call Ms. Bitchy Bitch Bitch from Bitchville. She always accused me and anyone else she felt threatened by with less-than-professional practices.

That's putting it nicely. Ms. BBB had a sailor's mouth. Every other word out of her mouth was "cunt," "fuck" and many other, "creative," coarse, harsh expletives you can imagine. You probably think you can come up with a doozy, but trust me, BBB has been there, said that and probably done it.

Her... ahem... *creativity...* would have been comical, were she at all funny. But no, Ms. BBB was always angry and shrieking at or about someone else. Her mouth really should have been declared a toxic waste site, and this, boys and girls is coming from someone who can go toe-to-toe in the expletive department, given the right circumstances. What I would have given for some guys in HAZMAT suits to come in and interrupt Ms. BBB during one of her tirades, spray her down and do a sterile cleansing.

Worse yet, she created an incredibly stressful atmosphere. One day she heard Aaron and me speaking about the Mint Jubilee and the fact that I was booked to be the Talent Executive—a promotion. It was all over then. That woman made it her personal mission to make my life miserable.

At Icon, I handled a couple of tasks: first, I was to cast a slew of extras for a scene in the show where MTV producers wanted to recreate the bar where Aerosmith famously played one of their first gigs in the early 1970s.

Shortly after I began that job, the producers found out that the band's kids wanted to be in the scene, and they asked me to reach out to the band to make the experience as seamless as possible. I wrote an email or two to Steven Tyler's then-wife, Teresa, and then got word from Aaron and higher ups at MTV that the band's family insisted they *only* wanted to work with me throughout the rest of the show. It made me feel pretty good.

When Ms. Bitchy Bitch Bitch heard this, she cackled for all in the production office (and down the hall) to hear, "Oooooh! Well! Ms. 'Talent Executive'! Look at YOU!" I don't even think she was listening to the entire story. She seemed to pick any random point in conversation to spew her chubby little insults (and yes, she was a chubster).

With the twenty or so extras I'd hired, my life on the show was busy enough. Don't ask me why MTV hadn't thought about feeding the poor extras I'd hired, whom they'd locked up on a soundstage at Sony, away from everyone else. Add to that the fact I needed to meet with the wives and kids upon arrival and check out their wardrobe, well that became a problem for Ms. BBB, who was in charge of getting signed releases from the band and their family.

The security was extremely high around the Aerosmith camp. Somehow, Ms. Bitchy Bitch was also in charge of who got into their area and who did not. She caused a very loud, screaming STINK over the fact I needed to meet with the band's wives and that *they* had made it clear it was only to be me.

"Well Aaron! You can go fuck yourself, if you think I'm going to let that STAR Stalker, Ms. (insert whiny sarcasm) *'Talent Executive'* into the Aerosmith dressing room area! You asked me to do a job, and I'm not going to take it in the ass for you, goddammit! I already have someone going in to get releases signed, so he can take care of it!"

Aaron was pretty useless here. I'm not sure what dynamic was going on between them. Maybe he had a female role-model issue from childhood or some other shit to deal with, but he was a huge disappointment. He remained silent, while I informed Ms. BBB that I had been assigned to meet with the band's wives and kids. I didn't understand what the big deal was and why she couldn't allow both her guy and me in, but she screamed, "Fine! FINE Lisa! YOU can go in then and get *everything* signed for us too! I don't care! I don't have time for your stalker bullshit!"

Yes. She was *that* ugly, and *that* deluded. I took the releases from her hand, turned on my heel and walked away without another word. I took care of everything with perfect professionalism. I met Steven Tyler and Joe Perry and got the releases signed. They were both super sweet and mellow. I went into the trailers with the wives and kids and took quick looks at the wardrobe. It was all done in a few moments. Everyone was so excited and happy. It was such a refreshing break from Ms. BBB, I secretly wished I could stay with them rather than go back into the shit storm. I dreamed of clinging to one of their legs and begging, "Please don't make me go back there!" And then I went back to work.

I still don't get what all the fuss was about, but I took care of my job and moved on. I had other fish to fry—literally, if I didn't get food for my twenty-some extras soon.

Once the show started, it was the usual mayhem. Get the celebrities where they needed to be and take care of business. One funny incident happened while I was escorting the Aerosmith kids from their seats in the auditorium to the backstage area to do their number. I had a couple of them with me, and just before we crossed in front of the widest row of seats to backstage, we were suddenly stopped. A jib camera was getting up-close and personal with none other than Pink, standing up from her seat, right in our path. I just stood there, staring at the camera and waiting for the moment when we could move, when I realized Pink, who was trying to dance and enjoy herself for the camera was looking sideways at me with a little concern on her face. *She thinks I'm stalking her!* I thought with a chuckle. *If only Ms. BBB could see this!* All was fine as soon as the camera left and we were able to pass, but I'll never forget that look.

Years later, I ran into Pink at a fundraiser in Malibu. I said, "Hi Pink. I worked with you years ago at MTV Icon. I'd love to get a photo with you."

She said, "Call me Alicia. What's your name?" She was very sweet.

Me with Pink, 2013

When the Icon televised portion was over, I was pretty beat. I went to the after-party, showed the members of Train to their private spot for the party, said hello to a few people from the crew and drove home. Then it was off to bed for me.

I am never one to blame anyone else for the defeats or losses in my life. I believe we make or break our own careers, relationships, and lives. Aside from child abuse, sexual abuse, or senseless acts of violence and terrorism, there are no victims in this world, only willing volunteers. But looking back now, I can see that the number of jobs I got with Aaron started to decline after this show. He had said his new mantra was the same as Mary J. Blige's: "No More Drama." This show had been filled with drama. I can now look back and point to this as the spark that lit a fire under Aaron's "no more drama" ass, and I can see clearly where he could have deemed me guilty by association in the menagerie. I had no way of knowing it *then*, because I still had a few upcoming projects to work on with Aaron, but hindsight reveals all too clearly how my position as "right hand" began to slowly slip away then. I am proud of myself for having the foresight to simultaneously branch out to other production companies for work.

It wasn't long, however, before I began to notice *everyone* "branching out" for work. The cloud of 9-11 still hung over the industry and that sense of desperation and scrambling over upcoming work began to be part of everyday life among most of my co-workers. I couldn't stand the desperate attitudes and behaviors that surrounded me, however. I wouldn't be bothered with anything less than positive determination. *I* would work, regardless of what was going on. I had no doubt about that.

Aaron and I still had the Mint Jubilee to produce and we kicked into high gear with regular meetings. As I mentioned, one year previously it had been the very first entertainment industry event I'd been privileged to attend. It was an annual fundraising event benefitting cancer. And this year, it was my responsibility as Talent Executive to work closely with Aaron (the Producer) to book talent for the show who would

a) perform for free, and

b) travel at their own expense—or at least, very affordably.

In previous years, the event's airline sponsor flew in the performers and celebrity attendees. Not so this year. After 9-11, we had no airline. I booked and made all of the travel, lodging and transportation arrangements for the performers, hosts and other talent on the show.

At this point I was a wise old sage, as these types of events went, and did not want to see a repeat of what occurred at the Super Bowl. So Aaron secured an assistant for me. She was a fun-loving, loud party girl named Kat. We became the best of friends immediately.

A funny scenario played out soon after Kat and I started working together. While prepping for the show, Kat and I worked from my home in LA., where she would make and answer phone calls and write emails with me. We would cook lunch and laugh. We had great chemistry working together. At one point Kat asked me how she should invoice Aaron for the show and it stopped me dead in my tracks. *Uh oh.* I said to her, "Oh, Aaron didn't tell you? This is all pro-bono. No one is getting paid."

She looked at me blankly, then half-laughed and said, "No! I did *not* know that!" and after a short pause she continued, "Well THAT'S good to know!"

Oh Aaron, I thought, *how can you* not *be open and honest with people?*

The true test to determine whether Kat was a sucker (I mean, LUCKY) like the rest of us, was whether or not she continued to show up for work. She did.

Hey, in *no way* am I at all ungrateful for the opportunities that Aaron and his friendly spirit afforded me on this great new path I'd paved. I'm just calling a spade a spade. Not everyone out there is as thick-skinned as me. But it was a pretty awesome path to be on, nonetheless. Everyone on the crew knew it and loved our time working with Aaron. We were all there for the paying jobs as well as the pro-bono gigs (even if we sometimes didn't find out we were working for free until after putting in two days or more). It doesn't, however, excuse Aaron from being irresponsible and disrespectful this way toward other colleagues and professionals. I try to go through life keeping it real and in doing so try to make no excuses for myself. The same applies to even the closest of friends and family. I'm an indiscriminate straight shooter, like it or not.

Kat and I continued to work on booking the show. We booked lesser-known acts, but it turned out to be an incredible event, nonetheless. The lineup included the alternative rock band Course of Nature, who performed a beautiful acoustic version of one of their best-known songs, "Caught in the Sun," with a local Louisville string ensemble. We also had country singer James Otto, a little known singer named Meredith Edwards, and Jamie-Lynn Sigler from "The Sopranos," who fancied herself a singer.

One day after we set up in Kentucky, while I was working feverishly from my hotel room to book acts, Aaron cried out over the phone, "Get me *Lit* Lisa!" And he didn't mean sauced on booze. He meant Lit, a band who'd become famous for their campy song "My Own Worst Enemy." Aaron and I use to crack up over their lyrics. I could *so* relate to kicking the living shit out of myself (you'll have to Google the song to get that one, because those mofos are hard to get ahold of for permission to use their lyrics).

So, work to book Lit, I did. It took me most of the day, but once I had them confirmed, Aaron decided to inform me he had no room for them in the lineup. I was livid. I'd spent hours trying to book the band he wanted, only to have him forget to tell me there wouldn't be room in the show? *What about* my *"no more drama clause," Aaron?*

"I'm sorry Lisa. I just realized there wouldn't be any time to load in and load out three musical acts, plus the string ensemble in our two-hour show."

These were just a few of the nuances I learned from working in production. To continue to work and be successful, you had to be able to keep rolling and not allow things like that to piss you off. I moved on.

The celebrities who basically made our event were those who came to celebrate with us and sit in the audience. We had Bob Costas, who also announced and co-hosted; Melissa Joan Hart, who can credit our event for meeting her husband and father of her three children, Mark Wilkerson, lead singer of Course of Nature; a couple of the Backstreet Boys; and Jerry O'Connell, who was still single and flirtatious as ever and had just come off the fun movie "Kangaroo Jack" with then-rising star Anthony Anderson.

We hosted other celebrity guests (many of them repeats from previous years), like country singer Brad Paisley before he was a huge name; Kimberly Williams, now his wife, then known for her show "According to Jim"; Brad Rowe; Jim Caviezel; Trista Rehn from "The Bachelor"; Sean Young as well as Shannon Elizabeth and her fiancé, Joe Reitman (whom I'd met the year before); Robert F. Kennedy, Jr.; Rachael Leigh Cook and more. It was quite a "celebrified" event, to say the least.

Two days before the event, the venue in Louisville was incredibly hectic. We had all the regular crew from the previous year: Antonio (and his girlfriend, of course), Brian and a handful of other regulars. It was loads of fun, but this time, because of budget constraints—again, after the attacks on 9-11, the fundraising and sponsors for the event had fallen off—most of our crew stayed in the town of IndyYucky, I mean Kentuckiana, across the bridge and over the border in Indiana.

That was another fun thing about the part of the country we were visiting: everywhere you went, they combined two or three words (or names) together to make new words, also known as *portmanteaux*. After a few VodkaTini's, we adopted the practice and made up our own names, like IndyYucky.

My mother and my sisters Jackie and Judy flew out to join the festivities. The day they arrived, I was ragged, frazzled, scrambling and unable to find a pen that would write or a printer that would print, let alone a space to work in. Kat was in charge of dressing rooms, so unavailable to me as a helper on site. Though Antonio's girlfriend tried to help, she was associate-producing the show with Aaron and extremely busy herself. It was pure mayhem.

Into the madness walked my sisters and mother. My sister Jackie announced from the doorway, "There she is! She is SUCH a BRAT!" You really must *know* my family to know this was all in fun.

The best part about the entire weekend for us, aside from the fantastic show we were able to produce, was the peripheral events. I was so glad to bring my mom and sisters along for the fun. It was basically a repeat of the year before with Britt, but this time, all the celebs, the crew and our guests had a private area in a local hot spot from which to party the night before the Jubilee. We were *all* treated like stars. Some of the best photos of my life with my sisters and mom are from that weekend.

Me, my mom and my sisters Jackie and Judy at one of the pre-Mint Jubilee festivities.

During that pre-evening private party, I joined Aaron, some of the executive producers and founders of the Jubilee and top celebrities. I sat with Jerry O'Connell and his dad for a spell. They were just casually chatting and Jerry and I began to make small talk when "it" happened. He laid the mother of all back-handed compliments on me when he found out how old I was (then 36) and said, "Wow! No way! Don't take this the wrong way (*uh oh*) but you are the HOTTEST *older* woman I've ever met." I should have flicked him on the forehead for that, but no. I laughed nicely and smiled and really did accept it as a compliment. Still, on the inside I was saying "I'mma bitch-slap you, Muh-thuh-Fuh-ggahhhh!"

Having two of my sisters and my mother there made the rest of the show a breeze. Granted, we had our share of mishaps and bumps in the show, but everything came off without a hitch, and the crowd was very happy with the result. We had a fabulous red carpet with loads of press documenting the celebrities' arrivals. Then once the show began, Kat and I frantically scampered across the ballroom, looking for celebrities who were needed backstage. We had to crouch so we wouldn't block the cameras' view. Because we were wearing gowns, we couldn't attach our walkies to our hips, so we had to hold them.

At one point, the manager of the James Otto band, Merv said "Wow, those are some pipes you've got there" to me—meaning my biceps.

I stopped, looked at my arms, shrugged and grinned it off. "Thanks! *I think!*" I said, "I'm trying to look glamorous here in my gown!"

The entire table all chimed in, saying it was a compliment. *Yeah, yeah... I know, I know. But why do guys like muscles on chicks? I'd much rather be lean, toned and healthy-looking.*

My mother, my sisters Judy and Jackie, and me in my headset at the Mint Jubilee, 2002.

My sister Judy was incredibly adept at scurrying around and getting things done, so I gave her a headset and put her to work. Finally, the show reached a point where Kat and I were able to take a mini break, so we snuck out to the loading dock to have a cigarette. I am not a smoker *at all* now, but back then once in a great while, it was quite helpful in alleviating stress or blowing off steam. It was also tempting if we'd had any drinks. Kat's joke was "I only smoke when I drink, but I drink all the time." But we enjoyed ourselves back in the loading dock and were able to flirt with more of the Course of Nature band members, who were also letting off a little steam.

Judy came to the dock. "Did you find Bob Costas?" she asked.

I felt like I was ten years old again, with my hand in the cookie jar as I hid my cigarette behind my back, smoke rising up behind me. "Not yet," I said, abruptly. It was pretty ridiculous to try and hide something like that from this sister who'd been a true flower child of the 60s. But family dynamics are powerful and my family was still trying to figure out where I stood on my Christian faith. Here I was drinking and smoking right under their noses!

I couldn't blame them for my neuroses. They didn't really know all that had gone on between Marcus and me, and certainly weren't privy to the role our church and friends played or didn't play. And they didn't know the kind of soul searching I'd been doing over recent years. But I didn't want to disappoint my sisters, who were both devout Christians. My mom, on the other hand, didn't care about any of that "born again nonsense." She only wanted me to be a devout Catholic.

There was always *that*.

Kat and I laughed a bit more on the dock and before all of our performers said good night, I went back in to say thanks and farewell. Merv, James Otto's manager, showed some interest in what I did for a living and gave me his card. He seemed pretty cool and was from New York, one city I'd not yet conquered (not that anyone ever does). Let's just say my interest in the guy was piqued.

I checked in on my mom and other sister, who were still seated at their table, and we all headed back to the hotel to rest up before the big race the next day. I was so proud to be able to host my family and provide tickets for them to the Kentucky Derby. I could hardly sleep that night.

Morning came too quickly and my phone started ringing first thing with questions from family and Kat: "Where should we go for breakfast? What are you wearing for the race? What does your hat look like?" Just insert question here: _____; I'm sure they asked it. You'd think we were attending the royal wedding, and truthfully, it's probably as close as we would ever get to such an occasion. But it was pure girl time and I could see that my mom and sisters loved it. That was all that mattered to me.

We placed our bets, bought mint juleps, snapped plenty of photos and took our seats for the big race. Aaron and the rest of the production crew were up in the expensive private boxes that I'd enjoyed the year previous with Britt, but Kat, my family and I enjoyed front-row seats, center track. We watched as the race winner crossed the finish line right before our eyes. I wouldn't have changed a single thing. We didn't win anything, but we had one of the most memorable times of our lives.

Jackie, Mom, me and Kat in our seats on race day (Judy, the photographer)

Our view of the Kentucky Derby, 2002. Not long after this, War Emblem—the horse making its way from second to first place—won the race!

That night we were invited, as the year before, to the home of socialite M.J. Diebold. Last year, I'd been romancing and flirting with Antonio, and this year I was footloose and fancy free. I was sad that Britt wasn't there with me again, but I was glad to have my sisters and my new friend Kat to cause trouble with. My mom, though she was close to eighty years old at the time, came with us to the all-night party and actually stayed awake most of the time, tapping her foot to the music and smiling happily as she watched my sisters and me dance the night away. We had so much fun, it was almost criminal. We danced with our fellow crewmembers and a few of the celebs cut loose as well. I don't believe we were able to rally people to sing karaoke as we'd done the year before, but it was a blast, nonetheless.

At one point, I was dancing with Joe Reitman, Shannon Elizabeth's man. Those who know me, know I have, well, this way of dancing sexy. I really don't do it on purpose, *really,* but I think every person has their own special swagger or dance move that is like a fingerprint. Once they learn it and get it down, that "move" or whatever permeates every dance. At one point, Joe and I were doing some kinda dirty dancing move and I innocently smiled over at Shannon, whose disappointment over Joe was apparent. I may be completely wrong, but it was enough to snap me back in time to when I was in junior high and would quickly straighten up my dancing act as the nuns passed by! I quickly unwound from my sexy strut move and reverted back to tapping my feet side to side and snapping my fingers. I would have no part of whatever *thing* might be going on there.

The last day in Louisville, the crew, Jubilee founders and remaining celebrities gathered at Joe's Crab Shack on the river for one last little soirée. My mom had a wonderful chat with Christopher McDonald, the actor who at the time was in a show called "Family Law" and was known for tons of other shows and films. He's now known for his work in "Boardwalk Empire" as Harry Daugherty and as Tommy Jefferson in the now-cancelled show "Harry's Law" opposite Kathy Bates.

Though we'd met the night before, my Mom brought my sisters and me over to introduce us to this nice Irish Catholic boy. It was so sweet. It saddens me now that, though they met once, she never had the opportunity to really get to know the man I now live with and love, who is a very talented, working actor, whom I call M.C. Nugget in the Ms. Cheevious blog. She would have loved him so much.

My family and I parted ways to return to our respective homes the next day. I went home to Graden and threw my arms around that cute little dude, whom I missed so much. I wrapped my arms around him and lifted him off the ground, pinning his arms to his sides. He loved it and giggled and wiggled, and then the dust settled for about a half a second.

I slept soundly that night before waking up to a phone call the next morning from Aaron for the "radio show." Once again we dished on all the characters and celebrities from the Jubilee and the Derby. Boy, what a cast of characters there. And what great memories!

Now it was time, Aaron informed me, to prep for the MTV Movie Awards. This was a big show for him and I would be only one of many on his crew (the Movie Awards I spoke of, where I met Tom Cruise, would come later). The show was less than a month away, so we were jumping in once again with both feet. Along with my colleague Brian from the Mint Jubilee, my role as Talent Manager was to help train the talent escorts—pretty people who were hired to help us. I also worked with Brian's new love interest, a sexy, cute little blondie, who was to assist me with talent credentials.

After hearing about the fun my sisters and mom had joining me at the Mint Jubilee, my brother Jim decided he wanted to try his hand at showbiz and planned to arrive smack in the middle of this production. Once again I put a sibling to work and I was glad he was able to experience the glamour.

It was hot outside during the day in our talent credentials tent. It was also fairly dull as publicists and managers came and picked up badges for their clients, the celebs and performers who were on the show. At one point, Jack Black, who was hosting the show, approached the tent. He'd just come off "Shallow Hal" among a few other fairly successful films and we could feel the tension while, flanked by a couple of bodyguards and reps, he descended upon our table. I was working on a side project as my assistant greeted him. I wasn't really paying attention until I heard Jack Black get irritated because she couldn't find his badge. I quickly turned, found the badge and handed it to him with a smile. He grabbed it and walked off in a huff.

I have no idea what the guy is like among friends and I'm probably being too kind here, but I chalk much of that sort of tension to stage fright or pure and simple pre-show tension. It still doesn't excuse him being a dick, but it's enough to make anyone tense.

It's funny. We assume these people, because they've acted in films and chosen this profession, should be totally on and find this kind of hosting a network award show easy-breezy. But I think we forget how unusual, freaky and frail many stars really are—probably even more so than any of us would be. So I shrugged it off. What did I care whether Jack Black was polite while he checked in? At least he didn't fawn over himself and choose not to go on stage on time like my friend Nelly Furtado. It's never okay to be arrogant and allow your reps to physically accost the crew, but getting a little huffy is to be expected from anyone in that position.

As the show kicked off, my brother had fun at the head of the red carpet informing our crew over walkie-talkies when the talent got out of their cars and entered the red carpet line-up. We instructed the escorts to bring the celebs where they were needed: teleprompter, a stage manager, their seat or whatever; celebrity guests and those who were not needed until later were all taken to the green room.

On shows like the MTV Movie Awards, celebrity managers and publicists often call the talent managers on a show, and it's vital to answer the phone. Once the MTV show was running pretty smoothly, I answered my phone and became engaged in a slightly flirtatious conversation with my new favorite music manager, Merv—remember James Otto's manager from the Mint Jubilee? Since then, we'd gone out on a date during one of his trips to Los Angeles from New York.

That was when I learned that he was married. At first, this was *not* something I was up for, but later I changed my mind. In my quest to live and experience life to the fullest, I saw this as a grand opportunity—a way to experience what a casual arrangement was like, a way to maintain control of my single life and possibly have some fun in the process. I justified it because not being officially divorced yet myself, I was in *no* position to become involved in *anything* serious, and well, that was it.

I won't speak to the other side of that issue, which is the family our tryst could be tearing apart, or the wife he was betraying. At that stage in my life, I believed we *both* made choices and I felt I was only living my life and he his. If it hadn't been me, it would have been someone else. Insert any other run-of-the-mill rationalization here.

I have since grown from that mindset, but at the time I saw my decision was only about whether I wanted to spend any of my time with him. Also, I truly saw this as one of those KEY "sit-ee-ations" I'd been looking for since Palm Springs, where I could try my hand at no-strings-attached dating. Plus, I was especially primed after getting "none" in Kentucky.

We were chatting away, with my headset hanging around my neck, when I began to hear faint but frantic screams from the earpiece. I hung up the phone and tuned in.

There was a desperate search for Kate Beckinsale underway. She and Ben Affleck had starred in "Pearl Harbor" just months prior. They were presenting an award, or nominated or something, I can't quite recall now. What I do remember is Aaron frantically calling out on the walkies for someone, anyone ("LISA!") to "FIND KATE BECKINSALE!" She was due on stage in minutes and hadn't yet done a read-through on prompter back stage.

I immediately put every talent escort on high alert, and sent my brother canvassing the halls. I was bursting through metal double doors, running down back corridors at the Shrine Auditorium, looking in ladies rooms and every nook and cranny. I went up to Ben Affleck and his friends in the green room and asked if he'd seen her.

"No...." he said, looking around slowly and calmly, as if to find her himself, "I'm so sorry. I haven't."

How do you stay so friggin' calm, when it's a serious emergency? I ran from him to search a nearby closet. My brother Jim, my talent credentials assistant (Brian's new love-slave), every talent escort on staff, were all in search of Kate.

Finally I got a stifled, timid cry from one of the few talent escorts to possess a walkie: "Lisa, I think I found her. She's outside, smoking a cigarette."

"Well, tell her she is needed." I started, but then thought better of it. "Never mind. I'll come there and talk to her. What EXACTLY is your twenty?" I ran through the double doors to the loading dock to find the elusive Kate Beckinsale, smoking and chatting it up with a security guard. Sounds nice, right? Awe, little Miss Beckinsale chatting with the lowly security guard, you say? No. Not when the rest of the UNIVERSE and MTV FRIGGIN' NETWORK virtually shuts down over her untimely need for a cigarette. I would have replaced her for less.

I'm sorry. Too harsh?

She had her own personal talent escort. We were all dressed in black wearing headsets and wandering all over the Arena. She could have let someone know where she was! It's why stars get paid the big bucks. If they don't want to do their job on *and off* camera—show up, be present and accounted for, and responsible to do what they agreed to do—then let someone else have the job. Just sayin'.

I went right up to her and said something like "I'm sorry, Kate but everyone is screaming for you and we've got about thirty seconds to get you backstage." She was sweet and obliged me as I basically dragged her ass (in her not-so-cooperative stilettos) to the stage managers.

All in all, however, the MTV Movie Awards was a grand event, with all the glitz and glamour anyone would expect. A-list celebrities and performers were everywhere. MTV always had what's called a "wet" set, which meant alcohol was served backstage, in dressing rooms and anywhere else celebrities may wander. If the talent wanted it in their dressing room, we made it happen. I'm sure there were some limits, but I'm not quite sure what they were back then. Things were pretty extravagant.

After the show wrapped, the green room kept hoppin'. The DJ was rockin' and everyone started to dance and drink to their hearts' content. I had to maintain a certain level of sobriety and professionalism as a talent manager. That didn't stop me from sexy dancing, (which you *know* I don't do on purpose) on the dance floor. It was a fantastic show and things went off swimmingly (at least on my end), if I do say so (aside from Kate Beckinsale's near-death experience). My brother Jim enjoyed himself and went home to New Mexico. My work there was done.

Afterward, I was faced with a long summer and very little work in view. On the other hand, it was summer in LA.

Jack The Dripper

"Before we talk about anything, I wanted to let you know that I lied about my age on my profile."—Big, famous film producer guy.
DUH.

I launched into summer by sending Graden off to New Mexico with his daddy. This was very uncomfortable for me. I knew Graden's dad would not likely be as tuned into the needs Graden might not be able to articulate, and not as nurturing. I had also sensed my little guy's heart struggle to feel safe and at peace after Marcus and I split up. Plus, my protective instincts were always in high gear around this time of year, when Graden would go off for a couple of months.

I worried his dad wouldn't provide solid support, but I also knew Graden welcomed anything he could get from his daddy with open arms. He was very much in love with him and there was no reason to fight it. I breathed in deeply as Marcus and he drove off to New Mexico and held it in as they were rounding the corner, out of sight.

In a gesture of support and to help distract me from all of this, Merv (my new love interest, who I'll refer to as M3 from now on, as in "*M*erv, the *M*arried *M*an") offered to fly me out to New York for a long weekend getaway.

I realize how uncomfortable this choice I made to have a relationship with a married man (or men) is for people. I understand that most people, though they may applaud the steps I took to change my life, frown upon my choices, especially if they aren't what they think are the best options. I can understand the compulsion to cry foul here, especially given the Christian world I'd come from and what that was supposed to mean. Hell, given the same situation in reverse, I know I would also be opposed. But I've fought my entire life against the instinct to offer unsolicited advice when I see someone doing something I think is stupid. I encourage you to read on, if this is you, regardless of your ideas about the topic of extramarital affairs.

This little getaway to New York served to open my eyes to the fact I'd somewhat over-romanticized M3 and all our relationship entailed. I began to realize that although M3 seemed like a successful, jet-setting music business manager on the surface, that definitely was not the case. He was going about his life, trying to make ends meet just like the rest of us, and it became obvious that I was not engaging with someone who had unlimited resources, or even close to that. Also, he was not shy to show his—how do I put this—*frugal* side? Yes, he flew me out to NY and he put me up at a hotel near his home. Frankly, I found the close proximity to his home to be a little strange.

I soon found that every promise of something "special" always had some strings or limitations attached. Was I surprised? Maybe a little. I've learned since that any married guy wanting to engage in an affair is only going to present the picture he wants *you* to see.

M3 didn't use his words to paint his picture. It was his lack of words. In this case, I said something like, "Wow! You're putting me up at a hotel on the Upper West Side? That's so great!" and he refrained from informing me that the *real* situation was not so "special" or anything to get too excited about. The room was tiny, without the space to even put a suitcase. Nope. Not even a closet or chair.

M3 also refrained from telling me things like "maybe you want to leave the big giant travel suitcase at home." He definitely knew I believed something else entirely and chose not to correct me.

It was a nice hotel, in its own way. It had been recently renovated, but it was also *obvi* that M3 had gotten an extreme deal here. I walked in and couldn't make my way around the room. I'm not kidding. It really was teensy. It was okay but did little to make me really *feel* the romantic, "forbidden love" adventure I imagined this trip would be. I felt more like the "hot little somethin'-somethin' on a budget" than the queen I knew myself to be. *Didn't he get what a rare opportunity it was to be with me?*

Let's face it. I'd met wealthy jet-setting men in my brief time working in television talent management. I'd obviously envisioned M3 to be one of them, so this was a little reality check. It wasn't that I was looking to be taken care of, or hoping he would shower me with expensive gifts. That had always been something I'd shunned, even from Marcus. But I wasn't all that understanding about this situation, because though I liked M3, there were other *single* men out there interested in me, who could also get me a cheap little room. I'd chosen him for the fun, exciting experiences the affair might have led to. *This* was less than fun *or* exciting.

My bubble was slowly deflating. I know, I know. I probably deserved it, right? I blame the movies! Where was my torrid love affair at the Plaza Hotel, and that diamond necklace to keep me from leaving? Stupid movies.

I sucked it up and enjoyed the getaway for what it was. I occupied my free time, which was actually a good amount, considering M3's—um—other obligations. I visited a gal pal who worked at MTV and met some musicians she was working with. We had drinks and had a great time shooting the breeze and shooting pool in Times Square. I connected with an old friend from New Mexico, who was now a ballerina in the city, and we enjoyed a dinner together.

The little alone time I shared with M3 was actually pretty great, I must admit. We had this incredible sexual chemistry—the kind you never forget. I don't know specifically what about it was so fantastic, as there were a number of things I liked about him. I was definitely drawn to the forbidden aspect. The fact that I didn't want any strings and had no desire to jump into a relationship with anyone was also appealing. And I was highly enthused about testing this theory of Sheila's that women could enjoy men for the sex alone and not become immersed or fall in love. I wanted to see if I could do it.

M3 was somewhat attractive in a distinguished sort of way, which is funny, considering photos of him from his younger adult days were that of a scrawny hippy with long curly hair. His eyes were a selling point. They were unique: almost an olive green and a beautiful complement to his olive skin. He had a Jewish heritage and definitely had that Mediterranean essence about him. He was pretty cool and his wardrobe was kinda' hip for a guy his age, mid- to late forties. He would show up to take me out decked out in his black leather jacket, dress slacks and a deep, dark jewel-toned shirt that made his eyes stand out. And I'd never dated anyone with an earring in one ear.

If I must choose one attribute that kept me hanging around, however, I have to say it was the sex. It was spectacular. That man made my body do things I'd never known it could do.

Aside from the hotel and despite his less-than-stellar circumstances and his annoying frugality, I had a really great trip.

One thing I can say about me, however, is that no matter how intoxicating, alluring, balls-out-hilarious or addicting the situation may be, I have a pretty good head on my shoulders. When it comes to making life decisions and doing what's best in the long run, I tend to come through big. I may divert from the normal course to experiment or try something new and exciting for a short time, but I don't typically lose sight of my goals and dreams for long.

Perhaps it's because I am pretty good friends with myself. Funny as that sounds, I *trust* myself to do a little risk taking. I really *like* myself, too, because I always come through for myself. I also don't have an addictive, destructive personality, I suppose. I was fortunate to realize the sex with M3 was sure to pull me in, if I allowed myself (or him) to turn this into more than it should be and that if I didn't safeguard myself against potential pitfalls, I would end up heartbroken.

When I returned home to LA, I decided to take a little detour in my dating life. I jumped headfirst into the online dating scene. Back then, I was braving uncharted territory. Online dating was akin to putting up a billboard announcing to the world not only that you were single, but maybe a bit desperate. It certainly wasn't widespread in 2002, but something being new and unfamiliar had never deterred me before, and it wasn't about to now. Did I ever care what the world or anyone else thought? No.

Most of my girlfriends would coyly or sheepishly ask things like "Have you heard about that 'online dating' thing?" It's funny, because every single one of them was apprehensive about putting their photos up and showing anyone that could possibly know them that they were jumping into online dating. I don't get that. What the hell did they expect to tell their family and friends if they met the man of their dreams? That always stumped me. I understand not wanting to "shout it out" until you're more certain, but I'm talking about people who were wondering why they didn't get dates when their online profile had no photos.

Today, online dating is commonplace. We all know about "catfishing," where people put up fake profiles. Sometimes gay guys masquerade as girls, or married people pretend to be single to fulfill some fantasy or engage with people they'd like to meet.

Back when I started online dating, the closest I came to a catfish situation was finding guys who put up a twenty-year-old photo or lied about their age. I'm sure more drastic situations occurred, but I was simultaneously brazenly honest and protective in my profile as well as my initial communications with would-be suitors. I was fortunate enough to weed out any possible catfish.

To my girlfriends, this new adventure only further cemented my reputation as a wild and edgy frontrunner. Telling friends the stories of my dates and watching their eyes widen in disbelief became a fun pastime.

I decided to cyber-stalk, I mean *date*, for a *few* reasons:

1. I saw it as a great way to keep myself busy and distracted, to ensure I didn't mistake great sex for being in love with M3.
2. One of my sisters had enjoyed some great times and met some wonderful men through online dating.
3. I needed to broaden my dating pool.
4. I love, and am authentically intrigued to meet new, interesting people outside of my own circle.
5. Let's not forget I was on a quest to live life to the fullest and remain open in my personal development.
6. It was considered risky! I was IN.

In case you haven't noticed by now, I have always been one to hear "a challenge to be conquered" when told "no," or where there is risk implied. I've always been game, always been the first among my friends to try new things. I don't mean that in the extreme sports or wild safari kind of way (though they are both on my bucket list), and that doesn't mean I jumped blindly into every new or risky thing. When I say I've been game for new and risky, I mean it in the gigantic, life-changing adventure kind of way—the kind of adventure that takes you out of your comfortable living situation and moves you across country, for no apparent or justifiable reason. Where, just when you finally feel comfortable in your own skin, your skin peels off and hightails it for another city.

Even as a kid, when things seemed too mundane for me, I would do what I could to change things up. When I was ten, I asked my mom if I could move to Pontiac, Illinois to live with Mom Hoerner.

"Why would you want to do that, honey?" my Mom asked.

"I'm bored."

"NO, you cannot move to Pontiac, Illinois to live with Mom Hoerner. There's nothing exciting for you there, anyway." Little did my mother know the kind of excitement I could create in a new environment. I always longed to find adventure.

While I often wound up taking those kinds of risks, it did not mean I lived for those moments, though I'm sure my friends thought otherwise. As my life progresses and I notice a new wrinkle, I mean *fine line* on my face, almost *daily*, I seem to let adventure pass me by more often than not. Still, adventure seems to hunt me down, and every once in a while, I still grab on and go for the ride.

This isn't to say that online dating is really *that* kind of adventure—but hey, in those days, it *was* to many people. So I read, listened and laughed at the experiences of anyone who'd gone before me. When I decided to jump in, I was pretty well versed on the subject. With a plethora of tools at my disposal, I made a list of personal rules I would strictly adhere to both online and otherwise:

1. Never allow a guy to come to your home, because then he knows where you live.
2. Never *tell* a new guy where you live, because then he knows where you live.
3. Don't get into a car with a new man unless you've gotten to know him very well and your friends know where to find him.
4. Never go back to his place when things are new (because then you'll know where *he* lives, and it may cloud your judgment). Wait until you trust him, and your friends know where to find him.
5. Tell the truth in your profile.
6. Answer every inquiry or email, even if you are not interested. Always be polite.
7. Never date someone who lies in his profile.

Of course, we all know that rules, even personal rules, are meant to be broken.

The first Saturday afternoon when I went through the somewhat simple task of setting up my online profile (it's no longer a simple task by any stretch of the imagination. It almost requires a Masters degree in Internet technology and/or psychology to be able to complete an online profile these days). Filling out the online "compatibility" form was a bit quirky and certainly one-sided. Being the marketing and PR maven I always have been at heart, I valued the importance of knowing my audience. I perused the profiles of some men I thought looked interesting and thought about how to write my bio. Working in entertainment, I thought it would be fun to meet and date guys in the industry.

I ended up with what I thought was a pretty well-written profile and uploaded my pictures from the Sheila E. event with Stevie Wonder and Sheryl Crow, only to receive an email from Match.com stating that "pictures of celebrities may not be utilized without express written consent."

Before I could even finalize my profile, I started receiving emails. Like, a LOT of emails. It was insane. I spent the rest of the afternoon and into the evening answering emails and perusing profiles to determine whether I wanted to have coffee or drinks with anyone.

One of the very first guys I met was a Latin lover type, who owned a sunglass design company. He was a very continental guy from Buenos Aires, full of great passionate expression. He was intelligent, artistic and successful. We had a great time together and I thought there could be potential for something lasting, even if only a friendship. We took to writing some very interesting and poetic emails between the times we saw each other.

One night, after having met him out several times and feeling a bit confident with him, I invited him into my home to have a drink after our date. We sat by the fire in the living room to chat and sip our wine, and it wasn't long before we started to kiss. I was enjoying myself and lifted my hand up to run my fingers through his hair. No sooner did I reach his hair line, or more like the edge of a piece of carpet, than he knocked my hand away and in a flustered, nervous gesture, got up, mumbled some random apology and left abruptly. I was a bit dazed, for a moment, not quite sure what had just happened. Then it started to click. I picked up the phone and dialed Sheila.

"Hello?" she answered.

"Oh.My.God. Sheila!" I said on the verge of giggles.

"What?"

"I just had a date with hair plug guy!" I said.

Shocked a little, but still chuckling in her somewhat annoying British way, Sheila quizzed me on what happened. We weren't sure if it was a rug, toupee or hair transplant, but it was such a great story and we laughed. Then, I determined I'd seen enough of that particular Latin lover. It wasn't because hair plugs, or toupee, or baldness or whatever were a deal breaker. It was the *way* it all went down: the way he obviously couldn't live with me discovering his great secret. The way he reacted. That was the deal breaker. I'm sure he wasn't heartbroken over it either, but that was fine by me. I had coffees and lunches-a-plenty on my calendar and I was only getting started.

Soon after that I met and had coffee with a very well-known film producer. He lied about his age in his profile. I should have been clued in when I arrived at the coffee shop to find a very worn, tired-looking man in his late fifties or sixties. The age on his profile: 45. I let it slide only because he was extremely intelligent. He said he lied because no one would even give him a chance if they knew his real age and this was his way of widening the dating pool. Can you say "smarmy"? I mean, really. Why not just get your dates the traditional way then, mister? If you can't nab dates in person, and you have to lie to get women online interested to go out with you, then maybe the universe is telling you something!

Despite all of that, we actually had an enjoyable conversation. Though he even looked older than his real age, he was a somewhat attractive man, so I agreed to go to dinner with him later that week.

Rule number seven—*Never date someone who lies in his profile*: BROKEN.

I won't lie here. I was a single mom with a son in elementary school. Money was extremely tight. I owned and lived in a condo that cost me over $2,500 a month plus utilities and homeowner's dues. I couldn't remember the last time I was able to take myself to a nice dinner, so the prospect of a nice dinner out with someone who was smart, successful—and an acclaimed film producer—had its own special appeal to me. So sue me. I deserved to be treated to a night out.

I said "Yes," and followed through. That is, until while on our dinner date, I found out the guy wasn't drinking because he was "sober." To that I said "Goodbye" faster than he could order another Roy Rogers. He thought it was odd that the lying about his age hadn't broken the deal for me, but his choice to live healthy did. Let me say this, once more, and with feeling: So sue me. I was never—repeat, NEVER—going back into a situation with someone who was an addict or alcoholic. No offense, but I'd been there, done that and it didn't work out well for me.

Whether he was an acclaimed producer or not, I ran out the door as fast as I could and went back to the drawing board on my online profile. This time I included a phrase to the effect of "Living sober, or recovering alcoholic/addict? Don't bother." What can I say? No one can ever accuse me of mincing my words.

Anyone with half a brain can tell from this episode that this area was a sore spot for me. I'd been scarred from the experience, but really, I believe we experience things in life in order to learn, grow and to move on when necessary. Life *is* the lesson, people. If we can't learn from past situations and move, knowing those things we prefer, cannot deal with, or won't deal well with, then there is no hope for *us*.

Listen. I am a health, wellness and fitness fanatic. I am all about doing what you have to do to be healthy physically, mentally, spiritually and socially. I applaud people who know themselves and don't compromise for others, and that includes sober living people. And I'm extremely proud of the very good friends I have who stand strong in their sobriety. But I am *me* no matter where I go and what I do. I exercise restraint, respect and honor when appropriate, but I do not compromise myself and who I am for anyone. Those days are over.

A few weeks later, Sheila and I went to happy hour with a couple of people whom I'd worked with during Super Bowl. We met at a familiar Hollywood stomping ground near Paramount Studios called El Coyote. Sheila and I noticed the place had a fair share of cutie-pies. There were a few at the bar and another two were enjoying dinner at a table close to our friends' table. Because the tables there were very close together, I was next to a cute guy and Sheila was next to his just-as-cute friend.

It turned out the guy next to Sheila was married to the chick who played Trinity in *The Matrix,* so we were immediately involved in what we thought was an interesting conversation about how much we loved the movie. I'm sure the guy was fed up with such talk, but we were certainly impressed both with him—and with ourselves for meeting such cool people.

I exchanged phone numbers with Dexter, the cute guy next to me, as he and his friend left the place, and then Sheila and I moved to the bar to flirt, I mean chat, with another cute young guy. You may recall her propensity for the young ones. She and her beau were still in that endless sort of on-again, off-again relationship and she was mid-off on this night, so it was a no-holds-barred-whatsoever situation.

Sheila was also trying to make healthy choices for herself. Just because she wished things would work out with her guy, didn't mean she would sit at home pining.

The same applied to me—sort of. I was still somewhat involved with M3, and when he came to town we would spend a few days together, but all other times, all bets were off. I had no intention of missing out on a potentially great guy because I was in lust with a married one.

I don't know if *any* part of this situation (or Sheila's, for that matter) could ultimately be called *healthy,* but as single women in the jungle, we did what we could with the resources we had. Everyone makes mistakes. We were making them happily, sometimes ignorantly, but moving onward and upward (psychologically at least) with each one.

Within a couple of weeks, Dexter called. I arranged to meet him for dinner and drinks out with Sheila and her beau, who were then mid-on. It was great to get him together with my good friends and be able to size him up in a different light. Dexter was super skinny and tall, a stereotypical artist type. He was cute with his messy bleach blond hair and blue eyes. Both of his legs together were probably about as big as one of mine, but I didn't care. I thought he was cool.

Sheila's beau fancied himself a chef of sorts, and one of his strengths was his great taste in restaurants. We met at some place in West Hollywood that had a fantastic chef. As dinner progressed, we began to notice that the restaurant was turning into quite the hot spot. A quick trip to the ladies' room, however, proved to Sheila and me that the men in this establishment were noticing our dates more than they were noticing us. This *was* West Hollywood, after all.

After dinner, I agreed to follow Dexter back to his place nearby for a nightcap. I gave Sheila the address and his phone number (never too safe in the big city) and followed Dexter in my car.

Rule number four, *Never go back to his place when things are new (because then you'll know where he lives, and it may cloud your judgment). Wait until you trust him, and your friends know where to find him:* BROKEN.

His place was pretty cool and cozy. He had good taste in furnishings and such, but not to the extent that I questioned his sexual preference (I know. *Stereotypical*). He was definitely still all-guy and he didn't waste any time showing me.

We were sitting in his living room, me in his over-stuffed sofa chair and he kitty-corner to me on the couch, when he basically climbed on top of me and started kissing me. I found kissing him to be enjoyable for, oh,... about three seconds. Then he drooled all over me.

He didn't stop there either. I crouched back in the chair with him on top, when he pulled back, up high above me, almost like an animal surveying his prey before eating. He was about a foot above me, when he literally drooled down INTO MY MOUTH.

It was all I could do not to FREAKING hurl my dinner right then and there—maybe even right back into HIS friggin' mouth! Would have served him right, too.

I ditched him as fast as my legs would carry me.

I quickly put the squeeze on that drool-monster's leak, squirmed to an upright position and politely issued the most obvious excuse to leave. I think I said something like "I just remembered I left my stove on" and ran out the door. This is where I happily proclaim my ÜBER, MAD personal skills. I remain a lady until the very end. I may be a freaked out, lying, run-away kinda' lady, but a lady nonetheless.

I called Sheila. I was holding back the vomit, "I just kissed him and he drooled all over me, Sheila!" She chuckled, sufficiently disturbed by this. We couldn't help but laugh. What are the odds? So I filed the evening away into my ever-expanding anthology of funny stories.

The summer was speeding by, and I had to get back to work. I networked and finagled my way into working again with Tony Cornelius for the Lady of Soul Awards. This time around, the regular transportation coordinator couldn't perform those duties, and fortunately recommended me for the role—something I'd never done before on my own.

M3 came into town for this because his client, Tony Award-winner Heather Headley, was co-hosting the show. She was quite "divalicious" (translation in case you don't' recall my Nelly Furtado story: not easy to work with) for someone with a new R&B album out, and who supposedly wanted to break into the scene.

M3 was perplexed as to why she was even in this business. "She's getting married or some shit," he quipped. "She's just not that into it."

Pretty funny coming from you, M3.

He was in town for a brief stint and then back out again, but the event was a fun way to usher in the fall and get ready for Graden's return home from his dad's. It was time to think about school supplies and nanny schedules once again, and boy was I ready.

My online dating adventures continued after M3 left town. I was getting my fill of coffee and drink dates with wimpy, arrogant, non-committal or simply *strange* guys. Hey, just because I didn't want a commitment didn't mean I wanted immature, flaky, weird people in my life. It was quite a trick to balance the ownership of my free spirit, while attempting to surround myself with winners. Free spirits, I learned, tend to attract flakes and bat-shit-crazies. A difficult tap-dance it was.

As we neared the cooler months of October and November, the next up on the dating docket was The Dripper, aka Mr. Dashing. This was a fun one. He wasn't *necessarily* the first one after Dexter the Drooler. He was just so much more newsworthy than so many others I'd met for coffee and drinks through online dating. It's funny how once you open yourself up to online dating, you meet new people and score dates *everywhere*. It's as if you've opened a channel in the universe simply by posting an online profile. I wish that worked for everything. If so, I'd create a site for people looking for millions in cash or something. Once you post your profile, suddenly millions of dollars from all kinds of places start coming your way, from resources you never imagined. *Ahhhh…*

I met Mr. Dashing (aka the Dripper) at Barnes and Noble on Westwood Boulevard. I bought a coffee and a magazine and headed up to the outside balcony to read and sip in the sunshine. I really needed the alone time. I'd left Graden at home with the nanny, Muriel, to run an errand and planned to eek out a little me time in the process. I was sitting there for just a moment, when a bumblebee landed on my table.

I'm allergic to bees. I froze. I screeched my chair back a few inches, eyes fixated on my enemy, when out of nowhere, Mr. Dashing took two long strides across the balcony and got rid of the bee for me. I looked up, a little embarrassed.

"Afraid of bees?" he said.

Well hello Mr. Aviator Sunglasses in Leather Jacket Guy.

I pounced on him—I mean, we struck up a conversation and told stories of our lives in Los Angeles: what we each did for a living, what we liked, who we were. He was a karate pro, who was "really famous, really, my pictures are all over the Y in Beverly Hills, I won all the championships. They all know me there."

Of course they do.

Eventually, our conversation circled around to relationships. He told me about his long-lost, forbidden love with his high school sweetheart, whose parents wouldn't allow them to date. I realized then how young he was. He was under thirty.

What was UP with these young guys hitting on me?

Aside from that however, he was cute, heroic, a pretty good communicator and really cool dresser.

He talked as though he was very successful. He said he came from a family with money and had gone to high school in Beverly Hills. I never really pinpointed what he did for a living that would have made him successful, but that's no surprise. In Los Angeles, you meet hundreds of people who drive around in very expensive cars, wear only designer clothing, and do about ten different things at once for a living. They're all mostly trying to make it big in their chosen field, or in *something, anything*. He had also been teaching karate at the Y, as well, and that was super cool to me. Anyone who was good with kids ranked high on my list.

We exchanged numbers and he asked if I'd be interested to go out with him some time. I said sure! I was really enjoying this newfound freedom to date around. I was also *loving* the fact that I could date more than one guy at a time and not be weirded-out about it.

Mr. Dashing moved *fast*. He called me before I reached my home—only a few minutes from the Barnes and Noble on Westwood Boulevard. I suppose I should have been a little surprised, but Mr. Dashing said his plans for the evening canceled and "would I consider joining him for dinner that evening?"

I know. He was a little *too* excited to date me, but hey, I was game for that. In my mind it was ABOUT FRIGGIN' TIME I received a little excitement and adulation. I didn't stop to think *Gee—perhaps there was something just maybe, just possibly a little tiny bit weird about this guy*. No. I couldn't see beyond the cute leather jacket and aviators.

When I got home, Graden was super excited to see me. Mr. Dashing was still on the line with me as I walked in the door. I started to try to bow out of seeing him that evening, citing Graden-time, when he said "Bring the little guy! I love kids!"

It would have been awesome if I had Ricky Ricardo around to yell some sense into me with his cute Cuban accent, but somehow I didn't. There was no one to say "LUCY! Don't be getting your pretty little head involved in this!" (If you don't know the TV show I've been referencing throughout this book, you are far too young and may want to do some research). One could argue I should have known on my own, right? But why? Why shouldn't I have assumed this guy was exactly who he seemed to be? That he was indeed a karate pro at the Y (and yes, they *had* heard of him), and that perchance he was simply astounded and mesmerized by my beauty, wit and charm?

I'm sure the question of whatever happened to "my rules for dating" is driving you mad right about now. But you see, I'd been applying them most of the time to men I met online. This is where things got confusing for me. I grew up in New Mexico, where almost every place I went, there was at *least* one person who knew me, or they recognized me because they knew someone in my family. I brought this sense of confidence, and I suppose safety and trust, with me wherever I went.

In most cases in Los Angeles, this mentality served both to assist my career and put me in imminent danger at the same time. If I met a guy in person, in the traditional sense, I seemed to find a way to break every rule known to man. All conventional wisdom flew out the window.

I actually *loved* the fact that I was one to take people at their word, for who they purported to be. I considered it to be one of my best attributes. But in this case, I wasn't quite street-wise enough to know better.

So when Mr. Dashing said "Bring the little guy!" I wrote it off as him being young and inexperienced with dating single moms. I now know the guy was, at best, highly insecure and probably extremely lonely and a little desperate, but that didn't stop me from allowing the guy to pick *me* up for an early dinner. Yes. I let him come and pick me up at my place. I know. STUPID.

Rule number one, *Never allow a guy to come to your home*: BROKEN.

Rule number two, *Never tell a new guy where you live, because then he knows where you live:* BROKEN.

As soon as I gave him my address, I told Muriel nervously about this situation. I gave her his name, cell phone, and any other information I had. I called Sheila and told her the situation and asked her to call me in ten minutes so I could give her the make and model of his car.

Yes, this is what dating in the big city is like, my loves, especially when your name *should* be LUCYYYYY because "you've got some SPLAININ' to do"!

Mr. Dashing showed up at my house while I was still going over things with Muriel. He tried way too hard to befriend Graden and sat down to play video games with him, asking him about all the newest games. I remember Graden saying something like, "I don't have that. It's only on Playstation and I have an Xbox."

Before Mr. Dashing could finish the sentence "Well, I'll just have to buy that for you," I said, "Oh no you won't! Goodbye honey!" as I stooped down to kiss and hug Graden goodbye and whisked this new dude out my door.

Dependable as always, Sheila called a few minutes later. I told her the guy's info and promised to check in later. No sooner had we gotten in his Ford Taurus than he asked "Before we go to dinner, do you mind if we run a quick errand?"

Rule number three, *Don't get into a car with a new man unless you've gotten to know him very well and your friends know where to find him:* BROKEN.

I'm a pretty easygoing gal, so I said, "Sure. But what kind of errand?"

"My business partner asked me to drop something off for him. This is his car, actually. I don't drive this kind of car. My car is a Mercedes."

Whoah-Geez! Here he goes again.

"Yeah. My car is much nicer, but it's in the shop. We won't take long to run this errand. I just have to drop off a package with a guy that works for us."

"Package? What kind of package do you have to drop off on a Sunday?"

"Oh it's nothing. These guys work all the time."

Shit. I should know better than this. I started frantically texting Sheila and Britt as I rode with Mr. Not-So-Dashing south on the 405. He talked constantly and seemed to be fixated on impressing me. We exited the freeway near Howard Hughes Parkway and I thought we were safe, as I knew of many businesses near the airport and assumed this was our destination.

"Are we going to a business near the airport?" I asked.

"No, it's this guy's house," he answered, glancing sideways at me.

He must have sensed the tensing of every muscle in my body, as he chuckled and said, "What? It's not what you may think. Well—what do you think?"

I answered him bluntly. "REALLY? Uh, it's looking like a drug deal! Hello!"

"No! No! It's not! I swear to you!"

"Really? So tell me then. What is it?" I quizzed.

"It's just this thing I gotta do. I have to drop something off to a guy."

I'm sure you do.

By this time we were maneuvering around a neighborhood very close to the airport. It looked just like something I'd seen in "The Basketball Diaries." I was *not* happy, but maintained my cool.

My date made a call on his cell that went something like this.

"Where you at? I'm on Market Street. (pause) Left? No? Right?" (makes u-turn after already turning left). "Okay. I'm almost there."

We rounded the corner and slowed to about two miles an hour. This was the kind of neighborhood where the homes were neat and tidy but were under the flight path. We saw a few people walking, but it simply did not look safe. I thought he was looking for a house number, when as we drove by, a couple of guys who'd been in the street talking, started toward the car, which was hardly rolling now. As we approached, Mr. Dashing rolled his window down and shoved a thick, rolled-up manila envelope out the window to the guy. He flicked his head back in what was probably his gang signal, for all I knew, rolled up his window and we drove off. I was frozen.

YOU GUYS, I WAS ON A DATE WITH JESSE FROM "BREAKING BAD"!

I must have breathed out audibly at this point because he said glancing toward me, "It's really not what you think."

"Yeah, right. You can take me home. *Now.*"

"No really! I swear! Those guys just work for me, and I…"

"Yeah, I'm sure they *do* work for you!"

"No! I mean, I just needed to get that over to them, but I *swear* it is not and was *not* some kind of drug deal or anything!"

"Then what the hell was it?"

"Just business, but please. Let me at least take you to dinner. Okay?"

Only me. Not someone else, no. The guy is the Lord of the Underworld, or at least Compton, and I get into his car. I break my own rules, and look what it gets me. Holy shit.

It was due to my deep-seated need and true desire to take people at their word (lesson learned) and the fact this guy was trying really hard, mixed with a little fear for my own safety, that against my better judgment I agreed. I figured the worst-case scenario was we'd be in a public place and I could call for help in front of witnesses.

We finally pulled in to the Cheesecake Factory. Stop the presses. I'm getting a little misty over this as I recall the joy I felt to pull into their underground parking at the mall. After a stunt like that, this supposed super-successful guy, whose real car is a Mercedes (and not the Ford Taurus we were in, *no*), chooses *the Cheesecake Factory* to reel me back in. FAIL. After a stunt like that we should have valeted his little beat up car at Spago or The Ivy in Beverly Hills.

We sat down after *all of that weirdness* to look at the menu. Let me just say, aside from the cheesecake, which I rarely allow myself the luxury of eating, I really don't like much of anything on the Cheesecake Factory menu. The food they offer is like one big giant combination of cream, butter, cheese, croutons, mac-n-cheese and deep-fried, breaded bacon, all combined in a peanut butter and jelly sandwich. Not really my cup of tea. Even their salads, when parsed out according to my diet, are about three and a half meal's worth of calories. It's kind of tough to make good food choices in that environment, so it made for a less than enthusiastic tone.

No sooner were we seated that Mr. Dashing excused himself to go to the men's room. *Now what,* I thought. And this is where he earned his new moniker: *The Dripper.*

He came back with a stack of paper napkins and was dabbing his forehead and neck. This guy was *really* dabbing. You'd think he just came out of a steam room. He was dripping in sweat. He sat down across from me and under the lights the sweat was even more apparent.

"Are you okay?" I asked.

"Oh yeah. I just sweat more than a lot of guys."

Yeah ... on coke!

"You're sweating. (pause) A LOT," I said, eyebrows raised.

"No, really. I am a super athlete. Do you know what that means?" he started intently, "It means my body is extremely lean. My body burns more calories than most guys, just by sitting here."

That is, if they're on coke.

"Looks to me like your body is *struggling* to just sit here."

"No. I swear!" he was defensive again. "I'm a triple black belt."

Uh huh.

"You can call the YMCA in Beverly Hills and ask!"

Didn't you just say this?

"My photos are all over the walls there, because I've won every kind of award possible! I promise!" A vein began to pop out on his forehead. "My body is just an efficient, *lean, mean fighting machine*, so I am always burning calories."

Yep, this guy actually said "lean, mean, fighting machine" with a sweaty, straight face. You have no idea the "super athletic/triple black belt" effort it took for me to not burst out laughing at that. I continued to get good laughs from it for the next three days.

"If you say so," I said.

I chalked up the entire string of events, including anything still to come, to cocktail hour conversation fodder.

I was miffed at myself and perplexed at how the hell I'd found myself, at thirty-some years old, in a predicament like this. Here I was: power chick extraordinaire, or so I thought, creating the life I'd always dreamed of on my terms, against all odds, kicking ass and taking names—and yet I, of all people, was somehow stuck on a date with *this* guy! Someone who put me in a questionable and probably unsafe situation, and was—well—a FREAK!

I felt like I'd stumbled down a long hallway, opened the wrong door and found myself in a slightly comedic alternate reality.

All I could think about was an escape route. I remember begging out of the movie (he would have kept me all night, if he could) and feigning some sort of Cheesecake Factory-induced illness (not too far off). I did agree to get a coffee at Starbucks in Westwood on the way home. It was wintery cold and foggy out as we walked down the block. I thought about how romantic the fog-covered streets and old-fashioned streetlights would have been with someone I actually *liked*. Then Drip-meister tried to hold my hand. I was disgusted. His hand was dewy, drippy and oh-so-sweaty. I shivered and withdrew my hand, because of the cold, of course. I should have been given an Oscar for my performance and was seriously thinking about that punch I never used on Mr. Punk NFL dude at the Superdome. But the most incredible part was, though it was cold and you could see your breath outside, Drippy "super athlete" continued to sweat.

Here I was freezing my ass off, wearing a beanie, scarf and coat, while he appeared to be overheating and losing fluid at an alarming rate. I was sure I'd have to call the paramedics soon. He dripped sweat from every pore on his body. Despite the frigid temperature, he went back into Starbucks to grab more napkins to continue the dabbing. OY VEY. I'd call it a comedy of errors, if it were at all funny!

When I finally arrived home that evening, I bid a quick adieu to Jack the Dripper and leaped out of his vehicle, never to return another call from the guy. I counted myself extremely lucky to be alive, let alone not completely *creeped out* beyond repair, and was feeling very maternal when I arrived home to my little guy watching TV. I made us some popcorn and sat next to him to happily watch Batman for the fifteenth time.

Mother Is Not A Four Letter Word

"No, honey, I'm not going out with my friends tonight. I want to go out with you! What would YOU like to do?"

Despite my decision to cut back on extracurricular activities several months back when I heard that adorable, heart melting voicemail from Graden, I began to realize *once again* that I'd slipped back into the grind (it was a fun grind, apparently). The first time I realized it and settled things down, it was Graden's sweet adorable spirit in that voicemail and in real life that brought me around. This time, his sweet, adorable spirit was... *misplaced*. His demeanor had changed ever so slightly. Anyone else may have missed it, but to me, he started to lose the infectious smile, adorable giggle and zest for life that were all a part of *him*. Truthfully, I'd been spending so much time pursuing my dreams it's somewhat of a miracle I noticed. As slight as the changes were, I felt horrible when I began to observe these changes in him.

Let's face it. It's the sharpest tools in the shed that find a good balance as parents and are still able to conquer the world. So here I was learning this lesson again. What does that tell you? I'd like to think I am among those sharp tools, but the journey hasn't been without the need for a little sharpening, as well as some real-life laboratory testing.

There isn't a parent on the planet who doesn't make mistakes or out-of-balance choices. Factor in single parents, and the "out of balance parenting" statistics are probably off the charts. Parenting is one of the most challenging, yet one of the most rewarding of life's responsibilities. But there is no guidebook for the decisions we parents are faced with, or how we should apply our decisions to each individual child. We can only try to educate ourselves, make our decisions, hope for the best, observe and try to rectify or make adjustments as we go along—in real time.

But it was clear that the most beautiful home, the best schools, nanny and neighborhood, though all great, were never going to be enough to make my child feel loved, safe, happy and contented. It was mommy that my son needed so desperately and I had been otherwise detained.

Let me be frank here. I know I've said it a bunch, that I'm not an idiot. Maybe I need to remind myself of that more often, but I knew all along that while I was out jet-setting around and working on television shows or fluttering about with colleagues, friends and love interests and away from my child, to him, no one or thing would ever be a substitute for me, the real deal. If you'd asked me about this back then, we would have agreed on this. I would have also launched into my spiel about how it was a difficult tap dance to be successful at work and be present at all times for my kids, especially as the sole provider. I would have talked about how doing what I love makes me happy, and that happy moms make the moms best equipped to care for their kids. I still believe that. I was always a very self-aware person and I tend to also be very aware of the emotions of or interactions with those near and dear to me, which is what I believe alerted me to Graden's less-than-enthusiastic demeanor in the first place.

When this all sank in, surprisingly the pain and anguish of the divorce returned with a vengeance and stung my heart anew. Though I knew

Graden was sad because of loneliness, I immediately recalled that he'd been so happy before the divorce and had Marcus never left, we'd probably still be together today.

The thought makes me cringe, but I couldn't help my sentiment. Relationships deteriorate for complex reasons, with layers of injustices, mistrust and betrayal. I also know there is no way to view things from a different lens, or peek into an alternate reality to determine whether a different outcome would have happened had Marcus and I never married, but I shudder to think of a life without Graden. Pre-divorce, it was clear to me that our home and family life, where daddy was king, was what Graden loved with all of his heart. In the midst of the divorce, even I had to ask myself if I were masking my own pain with distractions. But the pure relief and sense of well-being I felt when Marcus left was always very real, as the happy life I was leading now as a result was also real. As sad and painful as our situation had been, and particularly what it could do to my sons on a long-term basis, I'm convinced it was destined to happen. When our marriage ended and Marcus and I moved on with our lives, we were free to become healthier and happier than ever before.

On my own, I was doing what I truly thought was best for each of us—Graden, Joel and myself. With Graden's daddy gone, I had to be his everything: his breadwinner, playmate, nurturer, mother, chef, coach, tutor, disciplinarian and everything in between. I knew with every fiber that having a life beyond all of that made me sane and capable for the job.

As I realized once before, here it was happening again. My little Graden had lost not only his daddy in the divorce, but also his older brother (when he moved out); and now it seemed that once again, my little boy was grieving the loss of his mommy too. Ah, that whole "balance" thing. It's a juggling act for sure.

It was simple, really. Graden was in this new home, new school, new city, new everything, with no one he truly knew or loved to care for and nurture him. It is really sad and heartbreaking if I allow myself to dwell on it and think back to what was quite possibly a very lonely place for my little boy.

That was all it took, though: *that* realization kept hitting me between the eyes, helping knock the balance back into our lives again. There was no question in my mind. That little guy needed me and I was going to be there for him. NOW. PERIOD.

I approached this new realization like I would any project: head-first, with my full attention, balls-out energy and resources. So *what* that it felt like stuffing an obese woman into a size two girdle, by GOD our happy balance would be restored or my name wasn't Mommy.

To put it simply, I decided once again that the networking, events, nights out with friends, even my own personal adventures could wait, and it was time to restore the bliss. But how?

Once again, the usual response to invitations for nights out with friends, or networking events would be (for the most part) an unequivocal "No, thank you."

I also began working from home more often (when I wasn't on a set or a lot working on a show) and leaving or setting work aside early if possible, to pick Graden up from school. *I* took him for haircuts and on various other kid-errands. I'd always tried to accompany his class on field trips, but had allowed the nanny to take up the baton more than a few times in recent months. Not any more.

Baking cookies, watching kid movies, basically any of Graden's favorite pastimes with Mommy were once again *my* favorite pastimes. And exhaustion by tickle fight, hide and seek and basketball-dunking contests were all good enough reason to treat my little guy to a relaxing story-time-by-bubble-bath.

This was serious, and though I may have had a brief blond-spell, forgetting I'd learned this lesson already, once my eyes were opened, I proved to be pretty damn good at straightening up my act. I meant BUSINESS when it came to my kids.

I went out and bought myself a cheap bike and helmet, and Graden and I started riding bikes together. It became extra fun when Sheila and her son got in on the action. She bought the same bike I did and we each rode bikes with our boys the six blocks between each other's houses.

That Easter, we held an in-the-dark-with-flashlights Easter egg hunt inside Sheila's apartment, which was something fun and unique for the boys. I don't think they'll ever forget it.

Graden and I made more play dates and sleepover plans with friends at *our* house. I know. Me and *extra* kids—someone *else's* kids—at *my* house. It was pure madness. But actually, I *loved* it. The joy that returned to Graden's face and demeanor was irreplaceable.

I planned his next eighth birthday party to coincide with the release of the latest Incredible Hulk movie. Our part-time baby sitter (after we'd let the nanny move on to a new situation), Erin, whom Graden loved, joined us and about six of his classmates for the party and the movie. At the movie we noticed Michael Jackson and his entourage sitting in the back of the theatre. That alone was worth the price of admission, as every one of us in our row kept looking back in disbelief and awe. THE Michael Jackson! It was spectacular!

After a few months of concentrating on being mommy, as it always happens, another summer rolled in like a slow breeze. Graden was suddenly gone once again to see his dad for a couple of months and there was plenty of time for me to catch up on networking and adult playtime.

It was good timing because I'd begun to feel nervous about losing connections with colleagues and wanted to find more work in television again. I had taken whatever gigs I could get all along, but things were definitely different. I worked on occasional shows, but Aaron's emotionally-based hiring tactics, which I'd observed while I was his new star team member, had finally circled around to affect me, and projects with him had almost come to a screeching halt.

Simultaneously, I'd begun handling marketing for a local area cosmetic surgeon I'd met through Adrienne Maloof's then-husband. I began consulting with him and working from his office a few days a week. I was very fortunate for the unique situation it presented: I was able to work with him and continue to take on production gigs as opportunities came my way. It was a great scenario.

When Graden returned to LA, we jumped back into life as we'd left it. Fun times at Casa Davis. I took a short gig with the Lady of Soul awards, but that and my daytime marketing gig for the cosmetic surgeon were about "it" on the work front. It certainly made for a quiet autumn, which was fine by me.

For Halloween, Graden and I made plans with Sheila and her son. She and I dressed up as witches and decorated my place to be super fun and scary with cobwebs and a foggy, boiling pot of ghoulish stuff on the stove. We (mostly me really, the gigantic goof that I am) even cackled like witches and recited lines from Shakespeare's "cursed" play, MacBeth (*Double double, boil and....*). We had no idea about the "cursed" part until years later, so of course there would be no curse or mystical backlash. Right?

Sheila's ex, Antonio, and his girlfriend came over with another couple and their son and we all hit the streets of our neighborhood to take the kids trick-or-treating.

> What I am getting at here, by sharing this multitude of examples and what may sound to you like "Gee, look at what a great mom I really was," is that there are lessons here for everyone: You can make a huge difference if you simply pay attention to how your life choices affect the world around you, and how they affect your kids, your loved ones and YOU. Of course, you have to be willing to adjust as needed at all costs, but it can be done.
>
> Also, being a mommy (single or not) is not the restrictive prison-sentence people may think. In fact, it's the coolest, most adventurous ride there is.
>
> Relationships with our children can be and almost always are incredibly wonderful, but if they ever seem hopeless—like when the kids are in their rebellious teen years, estranged, or dealing with their awkward middle-school years—we can only trust and hope that the years spent snuggling and laughing, teaching,

prodding and rearing were not in vain. That they'll pay off one day, and big.

I feel joy and love from my boys, now more than ever, and it's a feeling I've longed to realize for many years. If I were to change any of the choices I made, I'd have to ask myself where I would be if I did, and how that would change who my kids are today? I love my kids the way they are right now. They are loving, kind boys who are quick-witted, street-smart and socially conscious. Would they be so great if we'd stayed in the OC? I don't know. The months and years after our move to Los Angeles weren't necessarily the easiest, but they were filled with excitement and good friends. And those years certainly churned out some strong, healthy individuals—myself, included.

Today, so many years later, I am still pulled back in time when I run across a photo of Graden with his big smile and remember his happy little hum, his precious little bowl haircut and his adorable clothes. Ahh, those were the days when I could dress him up however I wanted and he just sort of went along with it. Now that he's older, there is hardly a glimpse of that little guy. He was my baby. I loved and cherished his older brother deeply; Joel was my first born, and by the time I was living in LA, he was on his own for the most part, beginning his own life adventure. Graden, the cute little preschooler who openly greeted the other kids at school as we walked to his homeroom "Hey Timmy! Hey Suzie!" has become a young man who readily quotes lyrics from his favorite Rapper-of-the-Day on Facebook. I can still feel the awe and pride at the little guy he was with such a sweet, friendly demeanor. I miss him so much. I also enjoy who he is now for the whole new person I am getting to know. And so the cycle continues. But there are still no regrets.

I was never a perfect mom, but that was never the goal. I realize in telling all here, I've opened myself up to a flood of criticism: from those who are in the trenches now, and choose not to date or take risks; those who don't go out on the weekends with their girlfriends, or travel, or work in a field that takes them from their kids. And that is all okay. I would be surprised if there were no criticism.

We parents are a beautiful, unique and defensive lot. It's what makes us FABULOUS and highly skilled to protect our children. But I love my kids more than anything, and no matter what adventures I embarked on; circumstances and life-choices ALWAYS came back to that. My purpose always was and always will be about being good to my kids (and others) while being true to myself, and finding a balance in it all as I travel along my path.

Though I found a way to work in a dream-come-true field, and live in the city I loved, it was my life, my good girlfriends and watching my little guy Graden grow up and make friends that was the stuff dreams are made of. Joel was still working at the recording studio and was beginning to train in some other areas of the business, including DVD conversion. I was quite proud of him.

Things continued like this for some time. I worked my day job and the occasional entertainment industry gig, and I enjoyed being mommy to Graden.

As Halloween moved into the rear view and the holidays neared, I started conversing virtually, through my online dating profiles, with a few "eligibles." This time around, I branched out. I wasn't sure I needed to meet anyone in my city at this point anyway and I didn't want to be gone from Graden on dates more than once in a while, so I figured, "Why not?" M3 was from New York and that arrangement had worked nicely for a long while. So, I chatted with guys from Pennsylvania, Florida, New York, Aspen and a few other locations.

Hmmm, I could definitely get behind a trip to Aspen.... I'd always wanted to visit. This particular guy I'd struck up an online conversation with wasn't really my M.O. but it didn't stop me from entertaining a connection. I've met some of the most interesting people being open like that.

My girlfriends Britt, Sheila, Kat and a few others and I planned more often to convene our "girls nights," in which we cooked fancy dinners, enjoyed libations and (a few of us) smoked cigarettes now and then, while we chatted and laughed about our latest fling, love affair, work project, passion, or simply indulged in much-needed adult time. Ah, it was heaven. I loved those times and I'm quite sure Graden relished them as well. Whenever Sheila came over on a school night, it meant her son came along and was an instant playmate he hadn't banked on. He was happy to allow we girls our "alone time" while he and his buddy played games and laughed the night away.

I am a Mom... and I am also Ms. Cheevious
The memories of those years are from every corner of my heart and are the virtual locket I carry around. I've felt the sting in my throat as tears roll down my cheek for any number of painful memories and I've chuckled out loud often as I recall some of the hilarious and unique experiences I've had with, and without, my boys. Our life and times have understandably changed as both Graden and Joel have grown into young men. Graden and I lived new mommy and son adventures, some grand and some not, in LA and in other cities (one of which was Aspen, Colorado, but shhhhh... that story is yet to come), while various love interests came and went (and Graden reminded me that "baby" was *his* nickname, not some other guy's, on more than one occasion).

A few years ago, Graden went to live with Marcus. It was something he had always wanted, and I honored my promise to allow it when he reached the age of twelve (as unbelievably and impossibly difficult that was). My little boy's giggle has long since gone, giving way to the deep, crackled voice of a college-bound kid. I couldn't be more proud of him and of Joel—the two young men who define the most important role in my life.

But let's dispense with the sentimentalities, shall we? I am quite proud of the fact that I am a mom first. Being a mom is the best gig I ever had. But I am also every bit still that girl who sought to achieve whatever she could imagine as well. And I did it. I continue to do it. I'll never be too old to go after what I want. As they say (don't they?) "Forty is the new thirty." I'll just keep changing that saying as I age (fifty, sixty), because you see, life just keeps getting better.

I still work in the entertainment industry (some). I continue to work on select projects and am fortunate enough to attend some of the coolest Hollywood events ever. I've continued to reinvent my career and myself as time has rolled on. I'm a health and fitness buff, and a Pilates and yoga instructor, in addition to a publicist working with actors, producers, authors and more—in my spare time, of course. Despite all the challenges of working for myself, I love my rockin' life!

I'm incredibly happy to be able to say that I learned to snowboard and rock-climb. I have hung with Graden from a rope at heights that could make your skin crawl. I've tried things like wakeboarding as well as zip-lining, and some things I can't even name. I paint, write articles and blogs and I have made the whole social media world my bitch, way more than any *sane* person should. No really, I need help stepping away from the Big Screen—my computer. Most of these new adventures and experiences were just beginning *after* the memories recorded here.

My views on men, women and relationships have grown and expanded beyond what I ever envisioned for myself when I said "I do" at the altar so many years ago. My, how our little brains will expand and welcome new ideas, if only we let them. How could I know of the adventure and the balls-out wild ride that was in store for me? Certainly, I had no way of knowing how incredibly wonderful and rich my world could be that sad afternoon when I sat on the edge of my bed doubled over in gut-wrenching tears over the realization that my husband may be mentally ill, and my marriage was ending. Back then, I couldn't imagine a life that could possibly be better than holding my family together—which was what I wanted with all my heart. There was no way I could foresee the world that would open to me.

My trail has had its share of difficulties and struggles. Being a single mother is hard enough, let alone trying to do it with sex appeal, pizzazz and a little Ms. Cheevious. Add to that trying to find a way to make a decent living in the process and it seems impossible.

I've got a soft spot in my heart for single mothers. I'm convinced they are grossly overlooked as our nation's poor. I hurt for them because I know how overwhelming life can be. They are my cause and the reason for telling my story.

I love my adventures and I truly understand the value in taking risks, silly mistakes and mishaps considered. I am a testament to the fact that *I am the one person responsible for making my dreams come true.* Each person is, ladies and gentlemen. No one else is going to do it for you. There are always those on the road who lend a helping hand, but nothing is gained without our own determination, diligence, focus, personal responsibility and perseverance!

As for the dating, frolicking and my single-life adventures? Oh they continued—within reason, when I wasn't mommy-ing Graden or spending time with Joel. Perhaps those stories will one-day land on the pages of a whole *other* book.

But the mischievous, adventurous spirit remains my hallmark. I don't trade "ME" for anyone or anything. I am a single mom and I am Ms. Cheevious.

More of my favorite quotes:

"If you don't like being a doormat, then get off the floor."—Al Anon

"If you obey all the rules, you miss all the fun."—Katharine Hepburn

"You grow up the day you have the first real laugh at yourself."—Ethel Barrymore

"Happiness comes from good health and a bad memory."—Ingrid Bergman

ABOUT THE AUTHOR

Lisa Jey Davis is an author and the founder and principal of Jey Associates Marketing & PR, in Los Angeles, California. A women's health and fitness advocate, Lisa Jey is an award-winning writer, Huffington Post and Livestrong.com contributor and the author of "*Ahhhhhh … Haaaaaa Moments with Ms. Cheevious*" (a yoga routine in an eBook). She is a certified Pilates Instructor, Lagree Method Certified trainer, a Yoga instructor and a women's health and fitness advocate.

Lisa Jey's book *Ms. Cheevious in Hollywood* won Best Unpublished Manuscript at the New York Book Festival in 2007* and details with hilarity her post-divorce years navigating single parent life while pursuing a career in the entertainment industry. The book became the premise for her weekly blog/magazine *Ms. Cheevious—Bringing Mischief to the Masses* (www.mscheevious.com). The "Ms. Cheevious" blog along with various social media profiles (YouTube, Twitter, Tumblr and Facebook) sparked a widespread movement of supporters who follow the hilarious, indelible antics of a single woman and mother in Los Angeles, living her dreams on her terms, and despite the odds.

Prior to establishing Jey Associates, Lisa Jey worked in the world of entertainment television, managing show talent (Gwen Stefani, Sting, Sheryl Crow, Nellie Furtado, Dave Mathews Band, Stevie Wonder and more) for music based one-hour specials on networks like MTV, VH-1, CBS, (some specials of note: the NFL Super Bowl Bash, A Motown Christmas, MTV Movie Awards, ICON, Rock the Vote and many others). She continues to handle publicity for high-profile clients and events, produce television and new media, and book talent on select projects as time permits, and when she isn't shaping the booties of the masses in her hard-core Pilates classes.

Lisa Jey has written for publications and organizations such as The Associated Press, *The New York Review, Aspen Sojourner Magazine, Mountain Parent,* The Huffington Post and Livestrong.com (among many others). She has written television news and radio segments, as well as scripts for televised entertainment industry events.

Lisa Jey has spoken to thousands at conferences, shared her personal stories and hilarious anecdotes, and offered relationship advice and brutally honest truth to men and women about the opposite sex. A dating and relationship aficionado, she speaks candidly and humorously about it, as well as her life as a contented single. Her personal YouTube channel, "Enjoy Every Day With Lisa Jey" showcases her Thought for the Day segments (inspiring empowering thoughts), and her "Ms. Cheevious" channel offers comic sketches and commentary with special guests.

In 2011, Lisa Jey Davis was diagnosed with the BRCA2 Genetic Mutation for Breast and Ovarian Cancer. Her sister's seven-year battle with ovarian cancer (which took her life) was all the reason Lisa needed to take the most drastic approach to medical wellness: that of a prophylactic double mastectomy and breast reconstruction, as well as an oophorectomy (removal of her ovaries and tubes). She has since worked to raise awareness about genetic screenings and breast and ovarian cancer. Lisa is one of the go-to BRCA/Breast and Ovarian Cancer authorities called upon by the CW in Los Angeles (KTLA) for related news stories. She has appeared on the hit television show "The Doctors," as well as on KTLA in Los Angeles on more than one occasion, and on various other media outlets to tell her story. She's been quoted in regional print publications, newspapers, magazines and more.

Lisa Jey has another book forthcoming, now titled *Getting Over Your Ovaries: How to Make "The Change of Life" Your BITCH*. It is a witty survival guide for women dealing with hormonal issues and their own life changes, or those on the sidelines witnessing it firsthand and maybe suffering as a result. Her life's goal is to encourage others to be proactive in their health care and maintenance, and to learn effective, practical ways to live longer and healthier, and "enjoy every moment" in the process.

*Then titled *MILF This! Confessions of a Hot Mamma*

CONNECT WITH LISA JEY DAVIS and MS. CHEEVIOUS

Continue the FUNNY
Subscribe to the Ms. Cheevious blog to receive about one email a week with interesting, inspiring, or just plain silly or funny articles, here: http://eepurl.com/cwwWb
(You will also learn of book signings, speaking engagements and appearances by Lisa Jey Davis by subscribing, and you can easily unsubscribe at any time)

Connect with Ms. Cheevious here:
Facebook: www.facebook.com/iammscheevious
Twitter: @MsCheevious
YouTube: www.youtube.com/iammscheevious/
Google+: Search "Ms. Cheevious" plus.google.com/u/0/b/115350194416573230687/115350194416573230687/posts
Tumblr: www.mscheevious.tumblr.com
Instagram: www.instagram.com/mscheevious
Pinterest: www.pinterest.com/iammscheevious

Connect with Lisa Jey in social media:
Facebook Author Page: www.facebook.com/lisajey
Facebook Health & Fitness Page: www.facebook.com/lisajeydavis
Twitter:
AUTHOR @LisaJey FITNESS & HEALTH @BodyByLisaJey
YouTube: www.youtube.com/lisajeydavis
Google+: Search "Lisa Jey Davis" https://plus.google.com/u/0/b/112430035900410089840/112430035900410089840/posts
Instagram: www.instagram.com/lisajeydavis
Pinterest: www.pinterest.com/lisajey

SINGLE MOM RESOURCES

In the United States

(Searches for similar resources in other countries can be done on the Internet via Google or other search engines. You may also contact some of these organizations listed below for suggestions for help in your area. I apologize for the inconvenience!)

CHILD CARE

- **Child Care Aware**
  Child Care Aware is an information hub for parents and childcare providers, helping parents learn more about quality child care and how to locate effective child care programs. This non-profit organization offers educational materials to help parents accurately assess the quality of child care programs as well as a Child Care Finder that allows parents to search by zip code for local childcare providers and referral agencies.
  Child Care Aware: www.childcareaware.org/
  Child Care Aware of America (NACCRRA): www.naccrra.org/

- **Background Checks (for your baby-sitter, caregiver or nanny)**
  www.checkpeople.com

LEGAL ASSISTANCE

Find help with custody, child support and other issues at little or no cost to you.

- **Office of Child Support Enforcement**
  The Office of Child Support Enforcement partners with federal,

state, tribal and local governments and others to promote parental responsibility so that children receive support from both parents, even when they live in separate households. The national child support program is one of the largest income-support programs for families, contributing money to family budgets to help pay for the basics—shelter, food, childcare, transportation and school clothes. Child support makes a big difference to children.

Office of Child Support Enforcement:
www.acf.hhs.gov/programs/css

- **American Bar Association**
  State By State Listing of Pro Bono & Public Service Legal Services
  http://apps.americanbar.org/legalservices/probono/directory.html

MOMMY OR CHILD MORAL SUPPORT / ADVICE (GENERAL)

- **Parents Without Partners**
  Parents Without Partners provides single parents and their children with an opportunity for enhancing personal growth, self-confidence and sensitivity towards others by offering an environment for support, friendship and the exchange of parenting techniques. For the minor children of single parents, it offers them the opportunity to meet peers living within the same family structure and thriving. No more standing out in the crowd or feeling isolated because they are part of the single-parent family.
  www.parentswithoutpartners.org

- **Single Parents Alliance of America**
  FREE TO SINGLE PARENTS. SPAOA.org is a for-profit website comprised of information and resources for Single Parents across the United States. SPAOA.org is dedicated to the purpose of supplying third-party offers and information for financial aid, advice and services for single parents. SPAOA.org's efforts on

behalf of its third-party affiliates bring benefits including, but not limited too, medical benefits, financial aid, grants, discounts from groceries to clothing departments, as well as further education financial benefits, and serves as an industry forum for information and resources for single parents across America. We also include a full forum for members for support and advice. Members must be caring for and financially responsible for children at home. Membership is free to single parents who meet the criteria.
www.spaoa.org

- ❖ **Single Parents Network**
  Single Parents Network is a hub of collectively gathered single parent websites, articles, information, government resources, online discussion forum support boards, books and so much more, for any one looking for single parent information.
  www.singleparentsnetwork.com

- ❖ **Single Parent Meet-Ups**
  Search MeetUp.com for single parent support groups. They're in there! If not in your area, then start one!
  www.meetup.com

- ❖ **Big Brothers / Big Sisters**
  Moral support for your kids!
  Big Brothers Big Sisters help children realize their potential and build their futures.
  http://www.bbbs.org/

MORAL SUPPORT / ADVICE FOR PARENTS OF SPECIAL NEEDS/AUTISTIC KIDS

- ❖ **Through the Looking Glass**
  Through the Looking Glass is an organization that provides support to families with a child, parent or grandparent with a

disability.
www.lookingglass.org

- ❖ **Circle of Moms**
  Circle of Moms, an extension of PopSugar.com, is a website community that allows women to help each other. It helps moms in every situation of life through some of life's most challenging trials.
  They have support forums and groups for every area of motherhood, but **for single moms of special needs kids**: http://www.circleofmoms.com/single-moms-of-kids-with-disabilities-or-special-needs

- ❖ <u>ARCH National Respite Network</u>
  Need a break? Several organizations provide respite care to help parents of a child with a disability find an occasional opportunity to catch their breath. This website helps you locate respite services in your area.
  http://www.respitelocator.org/index.htm

FUN STUFF
Meet people, find kid-friendly events, and enjoy!
MEET NEW PEOPLE WITHOUT ONLINE-DATING:

- ❖ **Meet-Up**
  From wine-tasting to yoga at the park or canoeing down the river, you'll find a group of people getting together to do what you like to do on Meet-Up!
  www.meetup.com

- ❖ **Parent Meet-Up**
  www.parents.meetup.com (a different website from meetup.com)

- ❖ **Habitat for Humanity**
  Yep. Volunteering is a great way to meet people, and can teach

your kids some valuable life-lessons too!
www.habitat.org

- ❖ **Macaroni Kid**

  Macaroni Kid offers lists of kid-friendly events you and your kids can enjoy. They have a national site, as well as sites for events within your area. They cover most major cities.

  Macaroni Kid was founded with two very specific goals: enrich communities and empower moms. They call it "E2" and it is the driving force behind all that they do. They connect the libraries, schools, rec centers, community centers and all of the wonderful organizations and businesses that create programming and fun for kids and families with local families.

  They empower moms by supporting their Publishers and giving them the tools, training and the platform to build their businesses and be a force for good in their communities.

  National: www.national.macaronikid.com
  Search your city. In searching for Los Angeles, we typed losangeles.macaronikid.com and it auto-directed to the official page for Los Angeles: www.burbank.macaronikid.com

LAST-MINUTE BABY SITTERS
(pre-background-checked babysitters—for that unexpected date):

- ❖ **Sitter City:**

  You must be registered and set up in their system first, and it takes some time, so plan ahead.
  www.sittercity.com

- ❖ **Urban Sitter**

  Probably the same kind of set-up, although I've not ever used this

one.

www.urbansitter.com

- ❖ **Your Neighborhood Church or Private High School (not background-checked, so use your noggin' people!)**
  These places are rich for creating a solid list of babysitters to pick and choose from. Contact School or Church offices to place something on a job board, or to have people referred to you. Be organized. Meet them in person. Make your list of possible sitters and carry it with you. Be prepared!

www.ingramcontent.com/pod-product-compliance
Lightning Source LLC
Chambersburg PA
CBHW050632300426
44112CB00012B/1769